Praise for The Customer Driven-Culture

If you ever thought that creating a successful business was just about technology, then this is the book to change your mind forever. Travis and Monty take us into the guts of Microsoft to show how a "tech company" is actually a "customer-driven company." And creating a culture tied to practice was the key to making this shift successful.

—*Tricia Wang, Tech Ethnographer and Cofounder, Sudden Compass*

"If you like the idea of customer centricity but aren't sure what it feels like in practice, I can't imagine a better place to start than *The Customer-Driven Culture*. This book provides vivid, compelling stories about customer centricity in action--and specific, accessible steps to help you get there. Beyond that, it models the very characteristics of a customer-driven organization: openness, generosity, and gratitude. A treasure trove of great ideas, and a joy to read."

—*Matt LeMay, Cofounder of Sudden Compass and Author of Agile for Everybody*

The Customer-Driven Culture: A Microsoft Story

Six Proven Strategies to Hack Your Culture and Develop a Learning-Focused Organization

Travis Lowdermilk and Monty Hammontree

Beijing · Boston · Farnham · Sebastopol · Tokyo

The Customer-Driven Culture: A Microsoft Story

by Travis Lowdermilk and Monty Hammontree

Published by O'Reilly Media, Inc., 1005 Gravenstein Highway North, Sebastopol, CA 95472.

O'Reilly books may be purchased for educational, business, or sales promotional use. Online editions are also available for most titles (*http://oreilly.com*). For more information, contact our corporate/institutional sales department: 800-998-9938 or *corporate@oreilly.com*.

Acquisitions Editor: Melissa Duffield	**Indexer:** WordCo Inc.
Developmental Editor: Angela Rufino	**Interior Designer:** Monica Kamsvaag
Production Editor: Beth Kelly	**Cover Designer:** Karen Montgomery
Copyeditor: Octal Publishing, LLC	**Illustrator:** Rebecca Demarest
Proofreader: Christina Edwards, Holly Bauer Forsyth	

February 2020:   First Edition

Revision History for the First Edition

2020-02-21:   First Release

See *http://oreilly.com/catalog/errata.csp?isbn=9781492058717* for release details.

978-1-492-05871-7

[LSI]

Contents

This book is dedicated to three incredible leaders: Julia Liuson, John Montgomery, and Amanda Silver. And to the amazing people working in the Developer Division at Microsoft. Your hard work and dedication to our customers is an inspiration to us all.

How This Book Came to Be: A Note from Travis

There's a reason this book is titled "a Microsoft Story." Microsoft has played an essential role in the most critical and transformational moments of my personal life and professional career.

I was growing up in a small, dusty farming town in the center of California when computers started showing up as something you could buy for your home. During this time, no one in my family knew how to turn one on. Including me. It was my older brother, Ryan, who was the computer genius of the family.

One summer, he saved up enough money to buy a Compaq Presario 400 Series all-in-one computer. It came preloaded with Microsoft's Disk Operating System (DOS) and Microsoft Windows 3.1.

I was 13, and when he loaded Wolfenstein 3D and let me hunt Nazis in an underground dungeon maze, I completely lost my mind. It was the coolest thing I'd ever laid my hands on. I was hooked.

This was before the internet, so there was no "Googling it" when you had a computer problem. There was no one on YouTube to show you how to fix a corrupt *config.sys*. You did a lot of trial and error in those days, and only the persistent would survive.

Thankfully, I persisted. I struggled, shouted, and yes, probably even cried, but I finally figured out how to use the blasted thing.

Microsoft was there for the entire experience; from the Command Prompt, to the Program Manager, to Solitaire and Minesweeper.

I can still remember, way back in 1995, when I clicked the "Start button" for the first time.

I took advantage of the power of the Microsoft Encarta CD-ROM when completing school assignments, and I remember the awe I felt when Internet Explorer finally connected me to the internet.

In college, I used Microsoft Visual Studio and .NET to build my very first applications. Sure, they were simple calculators and command-line scripts that would make ASCII art using special characters, but the feeling of commanding the computer to do something I designed was profound and intoxicating.

When I finished my undergrad, I used Microsoft Word to draft up a résumé and was hired to work on internal ASP.NET web applications at a children's hospital.

Later, when I discovered the field of Human–Computer Interaction, I wanted to pivot my career in a completely new direction. However, there were no schools within a 200-mile radius where I could pursue this field in my graduate studies.

With the help of the internet, Microsoft Office, and a university tool built on Microsoft technology, I was able to enroll in remote learning and achieve a graduate degree from DePaul University in Chicago. I was able to access a world of education without having to uproot my family or move anywhere.

For four years, my brother and I hosted the *Windows Developer Show*, a podcast in which we would interview Microsoft developers and enthusiasts from all over the world. It was an incredible community to be a part of and truly inspiring to hear stories of how fans of Microsoft tools and platforms were driving the future of computing. Microsoft Skype played a fundamental role in allowing us to connect with our funny, brilliant, and inspiring guests so that we could share their stories.

In 2013, I was eventually invited by Microsoft to interview for a UX Designer position with the Developer Division (DevDiv).

DevDiv is responsible for most of the developer tooling Microsoft ships from the company. Chances are, some of the apps you use today were built by a developer using Visual Studio or Visual Studio Code. In fact, if you're using any Microsoft product now, there's a very good chance it was created using a tool built in DevDiv.

I'll never forget the day of my interview. A Microsoft Connector bus came to pick me up and whisk me to campus. These Connectors were everywhere.

I asked the driver, "Are these Microsoft cars and busses for employees?"

"Oh yes," he replied over his shoulder, "We'll take you anywhere you need to go, on campus and even into Seattle. Free of charge. The buses even have WiFi."

I couldn't believe it. I had entered some sort of metropolis of the future.

When he pulled up to the corner of Microsoft Building 40, I stepped off the bus and took stock of my surroundings.

There was a bustle of important and smart people rushing everywhere. The Microsoft campus was the biggest thing I'd ever seen. California State University, Fresno, where I had studied for my undergrad, was a third of the size. Microsoft's campus could've easily housed 20 of the hospitals I was currently working at, and probably had room for more. It was awe inspiring.

I immediately felt out of my depth.

When you're scheduled for an "interview loop" at Microsoft, it's a whirlwind day full of introductions, questions, and in my case, a design portfolio review and a "design challenge."

I met so many people that day. Everyone was gracious and kind, but they pushed me and challenged me at the same time. They were so cool and interesting and, about two hours in, I was desperate to work with all of them.

Out of the dizzying array of people I met that day, there's one person who stood out because he was simply impossible to forget.

He was a gray-bearded, tall guy who never stopped smiling.

Seriously.

He was smiling during my portfolio review, smiling throughout my design challenge, and smiling during my one-on-one interview with him. I remember thinking to myself, "Either this guy is smiling because he likes me or he's trying not to laugh because I'm a disaster."

When I finally met with him, we talked about literally everything. In a span of 2 minutes, he hit me with 10 books I'd never heard of, citing authors, quotes, and specific chapters that I "absolutely needed to stop everything and read!" because I would "drool all over it." I desperately tried to capture everything he was telling me. I kept thinking to myself, "I may never see this guy again, so I better remember everything he's telling me right now."

He had so much energy it was impossible not to feed off it. He was physical; if you said something that made him laugh, he'd slap you on the back. At one point, we were walking down the hallway, and he gave me a spontaneous high five. He made you feel special; but most important that day, he made me feel like I was exactly where I was supposed to be.

I liked him immediately.

Little did I know that day that the venerable Dr. Monty Hammontree would eventually become my boss, mentor, creative partner, and dear friend.

Monty has an affable southern charm; he's gentle but persistent and purpose driven. He grew up playing basketball, so he's competitive and will push you for excellence, but never in a way that makes you feel like you're not valued. If you find yourself in a debate with Monty, he'll go round for round with you, never once pausing for water or a towel.

There's no job too big or too small for Monty. He can be planning a wide-sweeping event for our entire division and still pause to vacuum our team room.

He's the "vision master." He's the guide that pulls you aside, points to the horizon, and says, "No one's looking over here, but this is where the gold is buried."

And he's right. A lot.

I know this because he's proven me wrong. A lot.

I've tried to describe my relationship with Monty by telling people, "He's the Doc Brown to my Marty McFly." Those of you who are familiar with the film *Back to the Future* might get the reference.

Emmet "Doc" Brown (played by Christopher Lloyd) is an enigmatic inventor who strikes brilliance by creating a time machine out of a DeLorean. Marty McFly (Michael J. Fox) tags along and gets to have thrilling adventures.

That's what's happening with this book.

I'll be taking the helm as narrator to share the lessons we've learned in how to move an organization toward customer obsession. Monty is the enigmatic inventor who saw all these lessons before I did. Without him, this amazing adventure would never have happened.

In the book *Multipliers: How the Best Leaders Make Everyone Smarter*, author Liz Wiseman talks about geniuses who make everyone around them smarter. That description fits Monty completely.

He has a way of seeing what you're capable of well before you do. He labels it and shows you how to harness and grow it. He pushes you hard, but only because he believes in your potential to achieve more.

Numerous times, I'd come into his office freaking out and in complete *imposter syndrome–meltdown* mode. I didn't come from some Ivy League school. I hadn't worked with the best in our industry. I didn't even have a PhD. I was a nobody from a town that no one had ever heard of. In a big company, where there's a specialist for just about everything, this can be terrifying. It's scary trying to find your unique value in a company of more than 100,000 employees. Working at Microsoft was a dream come true, and I was convinced I was going to blow it.

Thankfully, Monty knew exactly what my contribution would be.

He showed me that I could easily ebb and flow between technical, design, human interaction, and user research conversations. He demonstrated how well I understood the company, because I had been an obsessed fan all these years. He pointed to the work I was doing and said that, in the nearly 40 years of his career, it was "the best he'd ever seen."

He described how I was able to help teams understand abstract ideas by boiling them down to their essential parts. He pointed to all the people I had mentored and influenced over the years.

He said, "You're a generalist. That's your superpower. You help teams connect with their customers and each other. That's why you're here."

This was coming from someone who was on the ground floor of some of the most innovative work in user research. Monty is a partner-level director of research at Microsoft. This is a title reserved for only a select few user experience researchers in the history of the company. If someone of that caliber believed in me, there just wasn't any room for me to doubt myself.

Monty leaned into what I was passionate about. I had spent nearly a decade in my previous job as part of an organizational change movement to increase the satisfaction of our patients. My day job was in database administration and software development; but on the side, I would coach and mentor teams, teaching them strategies to better connect with one another and their patients.

I didn't think any of this was important. Company culture, team building, and organizational behavior had always been a side passion of mine, but I didn't see how that was going to be useful at a software company. However, Monty saw the bigger picture. With a new CEO, there was a strong desire to reclaim our purpose and be a company that obsessed over its customers. Monty knew how to exercise my skills just when the company needed them most.

As we worked to help transform the culture of DevDiv, Monty was patiently and persistently mentoring me through my own transformation.

Time and again, he showed me how to direct my energy toward these goals:

- Use a common language of learning.
- Build bridges and tear down walls with humility and a sincere desire to give my expertise away.
- Shape, mentor, and mold new leaders that embody the culture that you want to build.
- Be pragmatic and meet people where they are instead of forcing them where you want them to be.
- Help teams make the data they are collecting relatable to inspire others to action.
- Identify the vital behaviors necessary for culture change and how to measure them so that they can be repeated.

These lessons—what we call culture hacks—became the culture change journey on which we took our workgroup, our division, and eventually many other groups from all corners of Microsoft. Sharing these hacks is the purpose of this book.

There are so many other talented people at Microsoft who are working hard to help us all achieve a little bit more. They inspire me, and I am in awe of the people I get the opportunity to work with. Their work is a big part of this book, too. There are just too many people to mention them all here, but hopefully I've told them how much they've meant to me over the years.

I'm still that kid from that small, dusty farming town, but I'm humbled and eternally grateful to be the one who gets to share these culture hacks with you. I sincerely hope you find as much meaning in them as I have.

Figure I-1. Travis Lowdermilk and Dr. Monty Hammontree—yes, that is a wig (photo credit: Hannah Lewbel)

Preface

In 2014, at around 6:30 A.M. on a Tuesday morning, I was lying in bed and did what I always do when I first wake up: I grabbed my phone off the nightstand.

I saw a new email in my inbox:

From: *Steve Ballmer*

Sent: *Tuesday, February 4th, 2014 at 6:01 A.M.*

Subject: *Satya Nadella – Microsoft's New CEO*

I immediately jumped out of bed and began pacing throughout the house, heading nowhere in particular. I went downstairs, turned around, and went upstairs. Then I went back downstairs again.

"Whoa!" I shouted, "They went with Nadella!"

My family looked at me like I had lost my mind.

As I parsed every square inch of Ballmer's message, my mind raced through all sorts of compelling questions:

What does this mean?

What else is going to change?

How will Satya lead Microsoft?

It was exciting, historic, and completely uncertain. Less than a year after I had joined the company, we had a new CEO. The third CEO ever in the history of Microsoft.

This was a game changer.

It turned out that Satya had a core mission in mind: to drive customer empathy into everything we did. He wanted us to stop focusing on what everyone else was doing and recapture the core of what Microsoft did best: enabling our customers to achieve more.

To that end, 15 months after becoming CEO, Satya changed the mission statement of the entire company. Our mission now was to:

Empower every person and every organization on the planet to achieve more

The journey that has transpired over the past years has been a never-ending quest to capture customer empathy and customer connection in everything we do. Gone are the days of trying to "put a computer on every desk" or even the more verbose mission statement to "create a family of devices and services for individuals and businesses that empower people around the globe at home, at work, and on the go, for the activities they value most."[1]

Satya's call was simple and direct. The mission would center the entire company where it mattered most: our customers.

Later, he released a statement to employees and various news outlets. In it, he expanded on various drivers for success and the goals he wanted to achieve with our new focus as an organization.

Looking back on it now, one section stands out from Satya's communication:

> Perhaps the most important driver of success is culture. Over the past year, we've challenged ourselves to think about our core mission, our soul—what would be lost if we disappeared. That work resulted in the mission, strategy and ambitions articulated above. However, we also asked ourselves, what culture do we want to foster that will enable us to achieve these goals.[2]

In the Developer Division (DevDiv), we had already been on a journey of transformation. Visual Studio was moving from monolithic "boxed" software releases every few years to a rapid cadence of releases multiple times a year. It was clear to us that in order to remain competitive, we were going to need to decrease the time frame from when we had an idea to when we could get that value to our customers.[3]

This required us to shift our thinking, embrace uncertainty, and experiment with new things.

It forced us to make decisions much faster than we ever had before. We needed confidence in our decisions, and we needed to get feedback from our customers much more quickly.

The Hypothesis Progression Framework

Inspired by the Lean movement and Agile development practices, Monty and our team began to build a set of tools and templates—a complete framework—to help guide our product teams through quick and responsive ways to connect with and learn from our customers.

This work led me and my colleague, Dr. Jessica Rich, to publish *The Customer-Driven Playbook* (*http://shop.oreilly.com/product/0636920066606.do*) (O'Reilly). This book was designed to

---

1 [Foley]

2 [Bishop]

3 [Waters]

help our product teams move through customer and product development and quickly became the de facto software-making handbook for our division.

Using the *Hypothesis Progression Framework* (HPF; see Figure P-1), we ushered teams through the process of capturing their assumptions, formulating them into hypotheses, conducting experiments, and making sense out of their data.

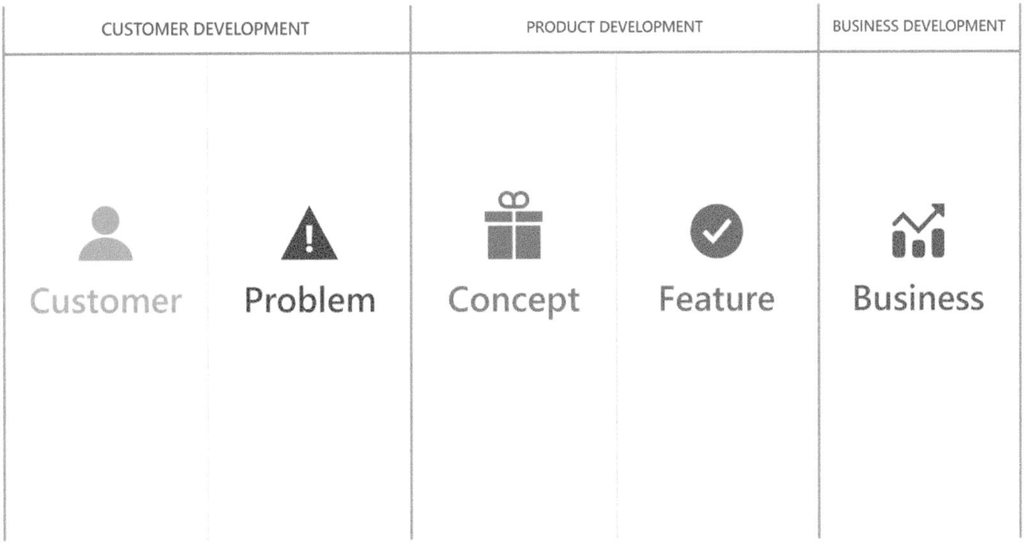

CUSTOMER DEVELOPMENT		PRODUCT DEVELOPMENT		BUSINESS DEVELOPMENT
Customer	Problem	Concept	Feature	Business

Figure P-1. The Hypothesis Progression Framework

Through these efforts, we went from a small team of researchers connecting and learning from our customers to an entire division taking on the role of researcher. Customer conversations skyrocketed, teams began to quickly pivot off of ideas that weren't testing well, and our teams were energized and ready to create new ways to drive less distance between us and our customers.

Essentially, our culture had shifted from a bunch of know-it-alls to a vibrant community of *learn*-it-alls.[4] What began as a simple set of tools to help our product teams gather better insights from our customers had gathered momentum and turned into a movement.

Almost daily, we were getting emails from within as well as outside the company with requests to talk about our book and to share tips and tools for driving customer empathy at scale.

We began to call the entire process *Customer-Driven Engineering* (CDE).

---

4 [Nadella] p. 97

Our learnings were spreading far beyond DevDiv and even outside the United States. Soon, our training materials were being used in Microsoft offices in Israel, China, and India.

To meet the demand of new employees coming into DevDiv every quarter, we began hosting "Customer-Driven Workshops," which walked employees through writing hypotheses using the HPF and talking to real customers. Soon, we were hosting attendees from all over the company.

We were thrilled with the reaction and energy we were seeing from DevDiv's customer-driven efforts.

Meanwhile, the company's stock had soared to an all-time high, and press articles were beginning to suggest that Microsoft was "getting its groove back."[5] It was clear. Microsoft was doing something radically different, and people were wondering what that was.

Our leaders were continually being asked how they were able to successfully change the behaviors within DevDiv. In a company of nearly 100,000 employees, there's a lot of ideas that get passed around. How did CDE become an idea that stuck in our division? How did DevDiv transform its culture and become truly centered on its customers? How did we get our way of working to go viral?

Essentially, teams were asking us what Satya was asking all of us in his email: "*What culture do we want to foster to enable us to achieve these goals?*"

That's exactly what this book will show you.

Who Is This Book For?

This book has been written for anyone who cares about their company culture. Perhaps you've been assigned to a task force or committee to improve an outcome like customer satisfaction. Maybe you've just started leading a new product team and you want to encourage customer obsession as a core focus for planning and development. You could also be someone who wants to improve their ability to inspire others to action by creating empathy and shared purpose in the work you're doing.

This book is for product makers who want to make exceptional products for their customers, regardless of what discipline you might ascribe to. If you're a program manager, engineer, designer, user experience researcher, director, or manager, you will find meaning in these pages.

This book represents a culmination of many popular themes in product making today: Lean processes, lightweight experimentation, continuous learning, and constant collaboration. Through examining our organization's cultural transformation journey inside Microsoft, you'll find new insights as well as some important validation.

---

5 [Konrad]

One of the unique things I get to do as part of my job is to interact with high-level customers as part of our Executive Briefing Council (EBC). Each interaction can be different depending on what the customer would like to see. Some want to have deep, technical conversations about infrastructure needs, others want to learn from how our teams develop software at scale.

However, a new theme appears to be emerging. As customers engage with us and discuss their journey through what Satya calls "digital transformation," it turns out that our customers aren't encountering just technical challenges; they're also dealing with very human problems. For example, a brick-and-mortar retail business that's struggling to meet the demands of online competitors might find that it not only needs cloud computing, but also a workforce that is willing to grow and learn to meet these new challenges.

The questions we are asked go beyond simple 1's and 0's, such as these:

- How can I get customer learnings funneled through our product life cycle?

- How can I push product teams to innovate and take risks?

- How can I inspire my employees to care deeply about our customers and less about shipping new features?

- How can I create an environment that celebrates a growth mindset and a willingness to adapt to a changing landscape?

- How can I get something like "customer obsession" to scale?

- How can I improve not only our customer satisfaction, but also our employee satisfaction?

- How can I influence others to change when the current environment in which we operate isn't sustainable?

What has become clear to me over the past few years is that digital transformation is *cultural* transformation. The two are inexorably linked. You can't transform your business by just moving it to the cloud. You must also invest in your people to help them grow and learn new ways of connecting with one another and your customers.

This book was written to address these questions. We've found that, in our own story, we've identified a common set of themes that helped us in our transformation. It turns out those same themes can be found in stories outside of Microsoft as well. Through these examples, our goal is to give you a concrete picture of what a customer-driven culture transformation looks like.

How Will This Book Help Me?

It doesn't need to be argued that creating customer value is good for business. However, what does it actually mean to be customer driven? It's one thing to say your organization is "customer obsessed," but what tangible things should teams be doing to bring customers into the center of their product making? More important, how can you achieve those key behaviors at scale?

This book is full of proven strategies that will not only inspire your company into the service of your customers, but also increase their overall engagement, improve their satisfaction at work, and fill them with a sense of purpose and direction.

The lessons organized in this book have not only been transformational within our work at Microsoft, but we've found countless examples in which they've proven successful in other businesses as well.

Bottom line, if you're looking for a practical guide that can transform your team or your entire company toward a culture that truly obsesses over its customers, this book is for you.

How Is This Book Organized?

Here's a quick list of what you'll find in this book and where to find it:

Chapter 1

> This chapter details the core foundation you need to build within yourself, your team, and your organization for cultural transformation to take place.

Chapter 2

> This is the first of our *culture hacks*. In this chapter, we discuss the power of language and how you can use it to inspire new thinking and behaviors.

Chapter 3

> This chapter details how to create an environment in which people share information and ideas freely.

Chapter 4

> To develop a learning-focused organization, you must create an environment that makes it safe to learn. In this chapter, we explore ways to encourage your team members to take a chance and learn new things about your customers and one another.

Chapter 5

> Your organization needs examples of what it looks like to successfully engage the new culture you're trying to build. This chapter explores ways in which you can build new leaders that exemplify new cultural values.

Chapter 6

To inspire others to change, sometimes you need to show them that you're willing to meet them halfway. In this chapter, we discuss strategies you can employ to get even the most stubborn detractor to consider giving your ideas a chance.

Chapter 7

When building a customer-focused organization, it's important that the stories of your customers permeate your everyday conversations. This chapter discusses the power of stories and how they can motivate entire organizations toward inspired action.

Chapter 8

It can be hard to measure whether a cultural effort is proving to be successful. In this chapter, we look at examples and ways to think about measuring cultural change.

We've also created some additional sections to help you locate the big ideas of this book. Be sure to look for:

Applying the Hack

Beginning with Chapter 2: Establish a Common Language, you'll find lists at the end of each chapter. These lists are a quick summary of the themes shared in the chapter along with ideas for how you can put them into action.

Agents of Change

Look for these sections throughout the book. These sections feature an inspiring story of change.

Books You Should Read

To write a book like this, you first need to do a lot of reading. In the back of this book, you'll find a list that features some of our favorite books on organizational behavior, culture, and leadership.

Useful Maxims

Monty and I love maxims because they represent little shortcuts to bigger ideas. This section represents a list of some of our favorite maxims, and you can also find them in the back of this book.

What If I Don't Work at a Company Like Microsoft?

Although the culture hacks in this book have been curated and refined in the halls of a giant software company, they're still applicable for any industry vertical. Whether you're a startup or a giant enterprise, a nonprofit or a government agency, you'll find something useful in these pages.

Essentially, this is a book that drives at understanding the building blocks that are required for a healthy organizational culture that is driven by the service of its customers.

Throughout this book, you'll find examples, not only from our division at Microsoft, but from retail, government, healthcare, hospitality, psychology, sociology, and many other areas. These stories will inspire you and provide a roadmap for how to successfully change the culture within your own organization.

Should I Read The Customer-Driven Playbook First?

This book has been designed to be a companion to *The Customer-Driven Playbook*. Essentially, *The Customer-Driven Playbook* gives you a practical process that helps teams apply customer insight throughout all stages of developing a product. It's a structured and detailed "process book." It gives you the actions your team can take to drive your customers into the heart of your process for making products. If you're looking for specifics on how to formulate testable hypotheses, organize experiments, talk with customers, and make sense of your customer data, that's the book for you.

However, having the appropriate process is simply not enough. To scale true customer obsession throughout your organization, you must consider strategies beyond employing a new process for getting work done.

In short, *The Customer-Driven Playbook* teaches you how to lead a horse to water. This book teaches you how you can convince that pony to take a drink.

Although we would highly recommend that you read both of these books, it doesn't matter which order you read them in.

What If I'm Not a Manager or in a Leadership Role?

A common question we're asked when talking about shaping company culture is, "But what if I'm not a manager of a team or in a leadership position at my company?"

In his book *Hit Refresh*, Satya says it best:

Changing the culture at Microsoft doesn't depend on me, or even a handful of top leaders I work most closely with. It depends on everyone in the company.[6]

Another way I've heard him say it is this: "You don't have to wait for your next promotion to become a leader."

What we've experienced, time and again, is that culture flourishes when everyone is invested in learning and growing. The thing is, you don't need anyone's permission to do that.

---

6 [Nadella] p. 120

"Be the change you want to see in the world" is often attributed to Mahatma Gandhi. Although it doesn't appear that he said this, here's what he did have to say about our own personal responsibility in being the change we want to see:

If we could change ourselves, the tendencies in the world would also change. As a man changes his own nature, so does the attitude of the world change towards him.[7]

We all have the power to influence the culture around us. In our day-to-day roles, how we interact with our colleagues and how we share our expertise and knowledge across disciplines or divisions within our company will have a dramatic effect on our own personal experiences as well as the experiences of others.

O'Reilly Online Learning

 For more than 40 years, *O'Reilly Media* has provided technology and business training, knowledge, and insight to help companies succeed.

Our unique network of experts and innovators share their knowledge and expertise through books, articles, conferences, and our online learning platform. O'Reilly's online learning platform gives you on-demand access to live training courses, in-depth learning paths, interactive coding environments, and a vast collection of text and video from O'Reilly and 200+ other publishers. For more information, please visit *http://oreilly.com*.

How to Contact Us

Please address comments and questions concerning this book to the publisher:

O'Reilly Media, Inc.

1005 Gravenstein Highway North

Sebastopol, CA 95472

800-998-9938 (in the United States or Canada)

707-829-0515 (international or local)

707-829-0104 (fax)

We have a web page for this book, where we list errata, examples, and any additional information. You can access this page at https://oreil.ly/CustomerDrivenCulture (*http://shop.oreilly.com/product/0636920283355.do*).

Email *bookquestions@oreilly.com* to comment or ask technical questions about this book.

---

7 [Gandhi]

For more information about our books, courses, conferences, and news, see our website at http://www.oreilly.com.

Find us on Facebook: http://facebook.com/oreilly

Follow us on Twitter: http://twitter.com/oreillymedia

Watch us on YouTube: http://www.youtube.com/oreillymedia

Building a Foundation for Change

Throughout this book, we focus on six "culture hacks." These are lessons we've learned on our journey of cultural transformation. These lessons, more than any others, have been the most profound and have given us deep insight into what's required to change the culture of an organization.

However, before we move on to those specific hacks, we must understand that they are effective only if you have a strong foundation in place. Culture change is like starting a fire, and, like a fire, the foundation is critically important. For example, I could teach you how to make a fire by striking a piece of flint with a piece of steel, but that would do you little good if all you had were a bunch of wet branches.

In this chapter, we explore the core foundational pieces that should be in *every* organizational culture. These are fundamental truths that show up time and again in every cultural transformation that I've personally witnessed or read about.

About the Developer Division at Microsoft

The Developer Division (DevDiv) is a division of nearly two thousand employees within Microsoft. It's where Monty and I work. We build developer tools for millions of customers that are, in turn, using those tools to build applications and services for *their* customers. It's a software development environment that takes advantage of the talents of engineers, program managers, designers, user experience (UX) researchers, documentation writers, business administrators, and many others. The story of our customer-driven cultural journey began in 2013, when we needed to produce software more quickly to meet the demands of an ever-evolving customer base. What became evident very early on was that we not only needed to respond more quickly, but we needed better ways to reduce the distance between the people making our products and the customers who relied on them.

DevDiv's primary product, Visual Studio, had been in market for more than two decades. In technology circles, a product division with that kind of legacy could easily be dismissed as a dinosaur.

Before our transformation, we had roughly 1.5 million monthly active users. That was a number we were proud of, but the overall market of developers we could reach was growing, and new pressures were mounting. Over the years, we were struggling to grow our audience, and new developers were no longer considering Microsoft developer tooling and services. To them, Microsoft represented their "mom and dad's company," not the company that spoke to the developers of the future. After many missteps in engaging with the open source developer community, we had found ourselves in a position with little credibility and trust. We were often seen as the "evil corporation" moved by control and greed, picking on the little guy, and squashing the spirit of the developer community. As the open source development movement flourished, we found ourselves outside the conversation, trying to get back in.

However, through our cultural transformation and the release of new tools like Visual Studio Code, we were beginning to see strong engagement with new developers who had previously dismissed our tooling. They were becoming vocal champions of a "new Microsoft." Not only were we seeing explosive growth for our new products, we were also seeing tremendous growth in our existing products. In short, existing customers weren't moving from our "old software" to our "new software"; we were attracting new customers to *both* products. We were experiencing a profound and exciting shift as we were winning over developers on every device, every platform, and every programming language. We were capturing developers' interest in our tools, even when they were building on our competitors' platforms.

DevDiv was coming back into the developer community, stronger and more relevant than ever before. We were beginning to earn our customers' trust back.

As of this writing, we're now at nearly 14 million monthly active users: 8 million using Visual Studio and 6 million using Visual Studio Code.[1]

Additionally, our Net Promoter Score (NPS), one of the many metrics we use to track our customer satisfaction with both products, is above 55. To give you a sense of the magnitude of these scores, based on global NPS standards, a score above 50, for any product, is considered "excellent."

DevDiv had proven that an old dog could learn new tricks.

---

1 [Greenwood]

The Culture Room

As word of DevDiv's success spread, Satya Nadella, the CEO of Microsoft, decided to visit Dev-Div to see what we were doing and determine whether any of it could be applied to the rest of the company.

Our team had spent months intensely focusing on answering this question. We had culled over our six-year journey, reflected on the prevailing research, and identified patterns to our approach that we believed, when applied consistently, had significantly influenced our culture.

So, we had a lot to share, but we had to convey all of this learning in 20 minutes, which was the time that was given to our team for his overall tour of DevDiv.

We decided that a simple PowerPoint presentation wasn't going to do the trick. For him to truly understand what was happening in DevDiv, he needed to see it for himself.

We landed on the idea of a *culture room*.

Effectively, we covered every square inch of one of our UX Lab's rooms with materials that represented the culture of DevDiv, as illustrated in Figure 1-1. There were testimonials; a 10-foot-wide banner of our Hypothesis Progression Framework (HPF); books that had inspired our approach; pictures of program managers and engineers interviewing customers; and a TV running video on loop of our "Developer Day" event, an annual event during which nearly 200 of our employees interview 100 of our customers in a matter of hours. The room also prominently featured the six culture hacks that represent the rest of this book.

Figure 1-1. One wall of our culture room

With it all assembled together, our boring, white, antiseptic lab had been transformed into an incredible exhibit that showcased the very best of DevDiv's customer-driven culture.

Before we share more about Satya's visit, let's look at the foundational pieces that were already in place when we began our journey.

These are important learnings for us, and they've become the essential bedrock for our cultural change. Before you can apply the strategies detailed in this book, you must build a solid foundation for change to occur.

The Foundations of Transformation

In Microsoft speak, we have the notion of "Priority Zero" (or as the cool kids say, "Pry-Zero"). I had never heard this term before, but when I first joined the company, it seemed like everyone was saying it. Finally, too afraid to look stupid, I pulled a colleague aside and asked, "What is this thing I'm always hearing about? This Pry-Zero?"

"Oh," she replied with a smile on her face, "that means, like, 'before we work on anything else.' It's priority zero!" Her eyes became large and she opened her arms wide to indicate that priority zero items had magnitude and importance.

"Well, why don't we just say it's the number *one* priority?"

"Well, because...we just don't. It's, like, even more important than the number one thing."

What I eventually came to learn was that labeling an action item Priority Zero became incredibly useful. Sometimes, you need to consider a foundation of understanding before you begin to add your piece to it. There are times when you must get the foundation set before you start on change. If you went to the doctor because you were desperately sick with the flu, you wouldn't appreciate it if he chose that opportunity to start a conversation about a low-fat diet. That's just not the right foundation to start that conversation.

As I stood there in our culture room waiting for Satya to arrive, I reflected on my own personal experience at the company. I thought about the foundation that had already been put in place in DevDiv (and the greater Microsoft) that created the bedrock for us to begin our transformation toward a customer-driven company. To understand the lessons learned from our journey, what would someone need to know first?

Thankfully for our team we were building on the shoulders of the great work of many before us. Leaders and individual contributors—throughout Microsoft and DevDiv—had worked hard to start the conversation for a new Microsoft to emerge. The following elements in this chapter represent Priority Zero. They represent the foundation you must pursue in order to have a healthy transformation of any organizational culture.

What Is a Customer-Driven Culture?

In *The Customer-Driven Playbook*, a book I wrote with my colleague, Jessica Rich, we described a process for performing lightweight experiments to better understand your customers and how to apply those insights to build better products. The book was written to help "de-risk" your assumptions and ensure that the products you build are useful and valuable to your customers.

Throughout this book, you'll see that being customer driven is synonymous with being *learning* driven. It's an ethos that states that the best way to serve your customers is to adopt a learning mindset.

In DevDiv, we earnestly capture our assumptions about our customers and formulate them into hypotheses that can be tested. We then run a wide array of experiments throughout the entire development process to ensure that we're validating or invalidating those hypotheses. What we've found is that when you constantly test your assumptions against real customers, you're increasing your confidence in your product decisions along the way. This prevents us from wasting valuable resources working on vanity projects or "solutions in search of a problem." In DevDiv, your feature, product, or service will not be shipped unless there is a legitimate customer need.

This requires our product teams to constantly engage with customers. We have state-of-the-art telemetry systems that help us determine user behavior in the usage of our products, but our teams still spend countless hours talking directly with our customers. This rapid learning cadence has been instrumental in our transition toward a customer-driven culture in which decisions aren't made by ego or politics, but what we've learned from the people who depend on our products.

LIVE SHARE: AN EXAMPLE OF THE CUSTOMER-DRIVEN APPROACH

An example of our customer-driven process at work is how we went about developing a feature called Live Share. Live Share enables real-time collaboration for developers when they're working together, but in separate physical locations. You might be familiar with a similar feature in Office or Google Docs that helps you collaborate with another user over the internet. If you've ever used one of these products in this way, you might have noticed your peer's cursor moving along with yours as you both edit a document. It's a fantastic way to collaborate with someone remotely, in real time.

Live Share works like that, allowing developers to follow along with one another while they code together on the same application or source code. They can also enter a debugging state in which they can work together, each from their own computer, to identify the point at which an application is failing. The value of Live Share is that, whether you're reviewing code with a colleague, working with a team during a hackathon, or teaching a classroom of students how to code, it has truly shifted how people collaborate when writing code—especially when they're distributed around the world.

However, when our product team began work on this project, it wasn't planning on building anything remotely close to Live Share.

The team began their work by investigating how developer teams engaged in rapid-release cadences. Together with our research team, our product managers were talking to customers who were building apps that required them to push out frequent updates and releases. As we had shifted to releasing updates to Visual Studio and Visual Studio Code much faster than ever before, we were becoming familiar with this landscape of software development. However, we needed to understand their problems so that we could determine whether we could offer them tools or services that empowered them to achieve more.

One of the unique challenges in working for DevDiv is that we're a division that is full of product teams that are building software for product teams that build software. It can be very "meta," and if we're not careful, it can be so easy to fall into a pattern of building tools and features that *we* want and falling into the false belief that our customers want those things, too. Many of our customers don't work on engineering teams that are as massive as Microsoft, so if we don't stay connected to where our customers are today, we run the risk of introducing features and complexity that are unnecessary or cumbersome. Additionally, for our customers that have similar needs to our own developer teams, they can compel us to push our products to new heights and sophistication. It's a tricky line we must navigate; to constantly push our products toward new futures, but not alienate the millions of customers that depend on our products to be reliable and familiar.

Thankfully, the Live Share team had been following a customer-driven approach. Over the course of a couple of weeks, the team interviewed 25 customers and had rich, vivid conversations with them. They learned about their work environments, how they were writing software as a team, and how they were using not only our tools, but our competitors', as well.

During those early interviews, customers were continually expressing frustration with basic collaboration. For example, when a developer asked a coworker for help on their code, the coworker was spending a significant amount of time trying to find the spot in code the developer was talking about, or, if the coworker tried to look over the developer's shoulder, they'd have to orient them to their developer environment. Things like the font used or the color theme applied to the editor could create a cognitive burden for the coworker who was trying to help.

It's like driving someone else's car: when you first get in, you need to adjust the seat, steering wheel, and mirrors to effectively drive the vehicle.

These situations would happen numerous times a day: getting up to speed with the configuration of their coworker's tools, identifying the problem and fixing it, and then having to go back and reorient themselves to their own tools and the problem they were working on. This constant back-and-forth was creating countless hours of wasted productivity throughout their week.

The entire product team was involved in exploring the many ways that we could address this problem for our customers. Product managers, designers, researchers, and engineers employed quick, low-fidelity mockups to express ideas and explore alternatives. During their brainstorms, they would diverge, creating multiple concepts, and then converge to narrow their ideas down based on stakeholder and customer feedback. Eventually, they came up with five significantly different ways to approach the problem of peer collaboration while writing code.

With those concepts in hand, the team reengaged our customers, walking them through the concepts and collecting their reactions and willingness to use them in their everyday workflows. At this point, no code had been written on our side, so the team hadn't become overly invested in any one of the concepts. This sort of "co-creation" embodies the growth mindset that we embrace in our culture in DevDiv and throughout Microsoft.

The team was skeptical about the Live Share concept at first, but the overwhelmingly positive feedback it received from customers when showing them the concept was undeniable. The fact that the team explored multiple concepts and that Live Share continued to resonate the most with customers gave our leadership team greater confidence that we had landed on a great solution.

The work didn't end after the concept had been validated as valuable—it had just begun. We had raised our confidence on the right *thing* to build, but the team needed to ensure that it built it the best *way*.

As the teams brought the concept of Live Share to reality, it fell into a weekly cadence, shaping each detail of the concept, testing various workflows with real customers, and then going back to make refinements. The concept evolved from basic, nonfunctional prototypes, to high-fidelity mockups, to working prototypes, and eventually to shippable code.

Building software this way honors the reality that without customer data and feedback guiding us, we cannot ensure that we're delivering on customers' unmet needs. It's a culture that requires us to check our own egos and be open and receptive to other points of view.

In my journey as a customer advocate, I've had many people point to Henry Ford's infamous, if apocryphal, words: "If I had asked people what they wanted, they would've said faster horses." Essentially, the thinking is, "We can't trust our customers to give us the information we need to deliver innovative products, because they don't know what they want. Therefore, it's up to us to figure it out for them."

As I just mentioned, it's under debate whether Ford actually said these words, but he certainly embodied this self-assured mindset.[2] Henry Ford's most notable innovations came from the fact that he was a ruthless optimizer, focusing on cost and price reduction. He invented cost saving and efficiently scaled mass-production schemes that are still in use today.

However, Ford wasn't known for being sensitive to customer needs and requests. A lesser-known quote that is also attributed to him is when he said, "A customer can have a car painted any color that he wants, so long as it is black," which perfectly captures Ford's thoughts on customer development and gives us insight into his hubris.

Compare this way of thinking to companies like General Motors (GM), a direct competitor of Ford. Its approach to manufacturing cars was to target specific customer segments. GM focused on understanding customers' unmet needs and landing on innovations like closed-bodied vehicles and new ways to purchase and finance a vehicle. GM released various innovations that were readily adopted by customers, allowing GM to gain ground on Ford and establish themselves as a worthy competitor.

By 1927, Ford was selling only a third of the cars made in the US. It eventually capitulated and started offering similar innovations that competitors had already been offering for years, and Henry Ford spent a lot of money retrofitting his factories and businesses to do it. Ford had lost its lead because of a false certainty that it knew what customers wanted better than they did.

So, what can we learn from the contrasts between a customer-driven mindset and a mindset that is driven by our own egos, and how can we apply that to building a product culture that focuses on its customers?

---

2 [Vlaskovits]

The Three Vital Behaviors of Culture Change

I love sharing stories like how our product team built Live Share by putting the customer into the center of its process. When I share stories like this, I'm inevitably asked a question like, "So, what do I have to do to get my product team to operate in this way?" In a sense, what people are looking for is a prescriptive set of steps—a one-size-fits-all solution.

I'm afraid that simply doesn't exist.

However, throughout our study of culture change, both inside and outside of Microsoft, we've identified three vital behaviors that are present when change occurs, at the individual, team, and organizational levels. These three behaviors are: awareness, curiosity, and courage, as depicted in Figure 1-2.[3]

As we talk about shifting your culture, we will continually point to these three actions as the core behaviors needed to succeed in any change effort.

Figure 1-2. The three vital behaviors of any change effort

Awareness, curiosity, and courage can be applied to any type of change effort, whether it be on an organization, team, or individual level. Let's examine how they can be applied to building a customer-driven culture:

Awareness

> Remaining competitive and striving for first-mover advantage can cause us to rely too heavily on shortcuts in our learning. We often do this by introducing our assumptions into our products and services. Most of the time, we do this unconsciously. Awareness is a vital behavior because we must constantly identify our assumptions so that we can

3 Credit goes to Sheila Anderson and Joshua Tabak, two superbly talented and resourceful program managers at Microsoft. They discovered these vital behaviors by examining patterns between our customer-driven work and our diversity and inclusion work. With their help, we were able to illustrate how awareness, curiosity, and courage, apply not only to how we should work with our customers, but to how we should work with one another as well.

formulate them into hypotheses to be tested. Only then can we move forward with any semblance of confidence that we're heading in the right direction for our customers.

Curiosity

To build products that your customers love, you must have a genuine curiosity about who your customers are. You need a desire to learn everything about them, from what motivates them, to why they behave the way they do, and what problems are preventing them from achieving their goals. Great product makers have a voracious appetite for learning, and they're constantly devising ways to learn from their customers. They make decisions by incorporating market reports, customer interviews, in-product analytics, usability studies, and any other customer data they can get their hands on.

Courage

When engaging in a rapid, constant learning environment, there's a good chance that you're going to be proven wrong. There will be times when you will be so sure that customers want your idea that it can be extremely unnerving to learn that they don't. Rather than becoming unmoored, you should be energized by learning a new way your idea *won't* work. Being customer driven means having the courage to pivot when customer data doesn't support your ideas or decisions.

We consider these behaviors vital because all three must be present for change to work.

For example, if you are aware that you're making product decisions based on your "gut" assumptions, but you're not curious enough to find a better way, you're not demonstrating the curiosity that's required for meaningful change to occur.

If you're demonstrating curiosity by investing in infrastructure to conduct lightweight experiments within your product but ignoring the data because it conflicts with the business model you've already invested in, you're not demonstrating the courage that's required to change your business as a result of what you've learned.

Hacking Your Culture

Culture is a product and in many ways, it functions like a software product.

Software is a set of instructions that detail how a computer should function given every possible situation. It takes inputs and responds with the appropriate outputs. Software also manages your computer's resources to make sure that it can deliver performance when given highly critical tasks. If software fails, your computer crashes.

The same is true with organizational culture. Over time, corporate policy and cultural norms shape the instruction set. A newcomer to the organization must "download" the culture to understand how to operate efficiently and successfully within it. And just like software, when a culture crashes, it threatens to bring the entire organization down with it.

So, if it's the case that culture is a product, we could certainly shape it by using the same customer-driven processes the product team used in making Live Share. In this case, our fellow employees are our customers. We can listen to them, collect their feedback, and adjust to meet their unmet needs. We can institute small-batch changes, test their effectiveness, and roll out larger changes when we have greater confidence in the outcome.

Just like a software product, we can "hack" our culture. Not in the "infiltrate the system and steal the valuable data" sense of the term; rather, in the hacker spirit of incremental experimentation, tweaking, debugging, and fixing. In the context of positive culture change, we mean hacking for good.

In keeping with this theme, the six chapters that follow represent hacks that you can apply to your change management process to make progress on your cultural growth. Our culture hacks are as follows:

1. Establish a Common Language

2. Build Bridges, Not Walls

3. Encourage Learning Versus Knowing

4. Build Leaders that Build Your Culture

5. Meet Teams Where They Are

6. Make Data Relatable

Through our experience working with countless teams and in different industries, we've found that these hacks create a culture that will help teams focus on their customers, unlock innovative experiences, collaborate respectfully, and engage their work with a sense of urgency and purpose.

When you consider hacking your culture, you're really ascribing to a mindset that is like the Lean engineering practices used in software making today. Lean espouses the virtues of moving quickly, adjusting as you gain new information, and continually pursuing new information in a close and collaborative way. You must apply this same Lean process to your cultural development, keeping what works and discarding what doesn't. Approach building your culture with humility and a desire to continually learn how to shape the path for your employees to grow.

Just like with product making, with culture building, you're never done. As your customers' needs and desires change the landscape of your product offerings, the needs of your employees will change the landscape of your culture.

Pursuing Purpose

Earlier, I mentioned how one of the first things Satya did in his first year was to update our core mission statement.

His goal was to illustrate where we should find our sense of purpose and our ambitions. To him, we would find those things if we were willing to recapture what had made Microsoft successful all these years. He referred to this as our "unique core."

In his email to employees, Satya laid out his view of the path forward:

> In order to accelerate our innovation, we must rediscover our soul—our unique core. We must all understand and embrace what only Microsoft can contribute to the world and how we can once again change the world. I consider the job before us to be bolder and more ambitious than anything we've ever done. Microsoft is the productivity and platform company for the mobile-first, cloud-first world. We will reinvent productivity to empower every person and every organization on the planet to achieve more.[4]

What was so salient to me that day was that he was calling for us to stop focusing on what Microsoft needed to do to win and put our focus on what truly mattered: helping our customers win. To do this, we would need to be aware of our own deficiencies, be curious and willing to learn new ways to help our customers be successful, and have the courage to put our customers' needs before our own.

What was so great about this call to action was that it was exactly the right focus for the company—at a time when the company needed it most. This email had been sent immediately on the heels of a major release of Windows 8. The reception to this latest version, a radical departure from previous versions of Windows, was lukewarm...to put it generously. The company had made a bet that tablet computing would be the path forward for our customers. Therefore, the product teams building Windows completely reimagined the operating system to focus on touch functionality.

Touch computing on traditional laptops didn't materialize as a strong consumer demand like we had hoped, and many customers were annoyed that they had to pay a premium for touch-enabled computers.[5] Combine that with removing the iconic Start button from Windows 8, and critics were knocking the company for being out of touch with customer needs.

Additionally, it was becoming abundantly clear that Microsoft was not making progress in mobile devices. Google's Android and Apple's iOS mobile operating systems were absolutely dominating the mobile phone space while Microsoft's Windows Phone operating system languished.

---

4 [Nadella] pp. 78–79

5 [Ranger]

In fact, a year after his shift in the company's focus, Nadella would make another dramatic decision by writing off $7.6 billion in assets to move away from the acquisition of Nokia that had happened prior to his tenure.[6]

With devices like the iPhone capturing consumers' attention, Microsoft had begun to obsess over the competition, pushing ourselves into spaces where we were not uniquely positioned to provide value. In our desire to be more like Google, Apple, and Amazon, we had lost sight of what made us uniquely Microsoft. Our focus had become fixated on what our competitors were doing and not on what our customers needed.

Many in the industry thought that Microsoft's worst days were ahead.

Nadella disagreed. To him, Microsoft had simply lost its way. Employees just needed to be reminded of our central purpose: to empower *others* to achieve more. That was the spirit upon which Microsoft was founded. That's what we were uniquely positioned to do, and in his mission statement to all the employees at Microsoft, that was what Satya was asking us to reclaim.

To build the culture you desire, it must center on a unifying mission that everyone can drive. The goal must inspire action, and it must be audacious.

Notice how Nadella asked us to empower every person and organization *on the planet* to achieve more. I like to think our leaders intentionally chose the word "planet" just to ensure that it covered every square inch of our world. We weren't going to just focus on business customers, governments, educators, healthcare providers, consumers, students, or small business owners. We were going to look for new ways to ensure that everyone could do their best work.

In his famous "moon speech" on September 12, 1962, President John F. Kennedy didn't stand at the podium of Rice University in Houston to ask the country to "consider going to the moon at some point." Instead, he inspired the country into action by reclaiming the nation's spirit and its desire to see the very best of what America could do.

In his book *Built to Last: Successful Habits of Visionary Companies* (HarperCollins), Jim Collins refers to these types of goals as *Big Hairy Audacious Goals* (BHAGs); they're clear and compelling and serve as a unifying focal point of effort. Collins writes, "A BHAG engages people— it reaches out and grabs them in the gut. It is tangible, energizing, highly focused. People get it right away; it takes little or no explanation."[7]

Having a core mission isn't just a rallying cry that inspires the troops. Research suggests that compelling goals have a tremendous impact on behavior, causing the blood in our bodies to pump more rapidly, our brains to fire, and our muscles to engage.[8] Compelling goals literally put our bodies into action.

---

6 [Warren]

7 [Collins] p. 94

8 [Influencer] p. 18

In our Customer-Driven Workshops in DevDiv, we ensure that each team receives a relevant business goal for its area to work on during the week. For example, a team working on Visual Studio might be assigned a goal like, "Triple the number of Python developers using Visual Studio as their primary editor over the next six months." Trust me, this is audacious. We don't have workshop attendees work on superfluous goals that are meaningless. We don't say, "Okay. For the next four days, each team will design a better bike helmet." Sure, if our group was responsible for helping Microsoft make better bike helmets, this could be a great goal, but we work on tools for developers.

Because our workshop attendees are given an audacious business goal for which they are directly responsible, we achieve much more engagement and commitment in our workshops. Our workshops aren't seen as "required training"; rather, they're an opportunity to generate real career capital and solve real problems.

Younger employees—for some of whom Microsoft is their first job out of college—really latch on to these challenges. Millennials, the generation of employees born between 1980 and 2005, have become the nation's largest workforce. Numerous surveys of these 82 million young workers have suggested that they place far greater emphasis on purpose, passion, and meaning in their work.[9] Although a competitive salary is still important, millennials will also leave jobs where they are unable to connect their own purpose with the organization's greater mission.

The point here is that, to galvanize a group of people and drive a culture change, you must rally them around a core goal that is immediately accessible and audacious enough to push them farther than they ever thought possible.

Kathleen Hogan, Microsoft's executive vice president of human resources, says that purpose is what helps her lead, even in challenging times.

"Sometimes, leadership is hard," she says. "But having that sense that what you are doing is something you deeply care about, that's what I lean on when I have days when I think 'we are not delivering.' Coming back to that purpose and why this work matters, that is key to propelling you forward in your journey as a leader."[10]

Diversity and Inclusion

To build a culture that serves the ever-changing and diverse needs of your customers, your organization must reflect the same level of diversity in its workforce. You simply cannot discuss building a strong culture without addressing the need for diverse backgrounds, perspectives, and voices.

---

9 [Field]

10 [Bulgarella]

Numerous studies show that diverse teams perform better,[11] are more creative,[12] and make more ethical decisions.[13]

So why then do organizations struggle with creating a diverse workforce?

Microsoft has certainly had its own missteps as it tries to create a more diverse company. In 2019, an internal email thread leaked to the press, detailing numerous stories of harassment and inappropriate behavior that women at Microsoft were experiencing.[14] The stories were horrifying, and it was clear that our plan to be a diverse and inclusive technology company was not working. Many employees were outraged and demanded that Satya and other leaders at the company address the claims of discrimination and harassment much more quickly. Urgent action was needed.

For me, watching our leaders respond to these issues has been painful, but also inspiring and informative. It was incredibly difficult to hear those stories, and it was hard not to be disappointed. However, by listening to these employees and leaning in, I was able to confront my own unconscious biases as well as own that my positive experience at Microsoft hasn't been shared by everyone, particularly those in underrepresented groups like women and people of color. It was an important learning and I'm grateful for it.

Despite our best intentions, it's human nature to seek homogeneity and harmony within our workgroups. We seek confirmation of our beliefs and often gravitate to those with similar backgrounds, experiences, and thinking. We like people who have the same sense of humor as us, like the same things we like, and have similar opinions to our own.

The challenge is that these implicit biases could be excluding voices and experiences that are different from our own for the sake of expediency or to avoid conflict. Therefore, we must remain aware of and act against those biases to prevent them from weaving their way into our day-to-day working interactions.

Amanda Silver, partner director of program management in DevDiv, says that diversity and inclusion is about the three aforementioned vital behaviors: awareness, curiosity, and courage.[15]

Silver says that these behaviors show up in the context of everyday situations. One example she describes is a meeting in which you have half the team members physically present and the other half dialing in remotely over the phone.

"[In these situations], what is the order of operations that you must have to ensure that every voice is heard and that there's not a power dynamic?" Silver asks, pointing to the clear

---

11 [Richard]

12 [McLeod]

13 [DeGrassi]

14 [Tiku]

15 [Silver-1]

advantage team members have when they're physically present in meetings. They can read body language and interject much more easily than those dialing in over the phone.

"Everyone can relate to this. This isn't just about gender, ethnicity, or class," she says. "Some people are physically present, and some people are remote, and you have to make accommodations to ensure that remote people are included in the conversation."

To Amanda, these situations require awareness that there are people in the meeting who cannot be seen.

She says it also requires curiosity: you need to check in with remote members to ensure that they're not having a difficult time interjecting into the conversation.

"So, what you do," she continues, "is you naturally build in pauses into the conversation and you do checkpoints, where you ask questions [of remote members]. You intentionally call on the people that have been silent to make sure they have an opportunity for their voice to be heard. [As a leader], your job is to make the room for everyone else on your team," she says.

Amanda uses the remote meeting as just one minor but meaningful example of how she shows up as a leader. She exhibits the three vital behaviors, not just for remote employees, but she also points to how they can be helpful in accommodating other differences. For example, she says that people who are generally more introverted also need more time to process and reply, just like remote employees. They're easily overlooked if she's unwilling to check in with them and ask them questions.

What makes Amanda an exceptional leader is that she models a learning culture by applying awareness and curiosity to her leadership style, continually looking for ways to better engage her team and uncover the best ideas.

Finally, she says that behaving in this way requires courage.

"It takes courage to let someone else speak," she admits, "because you might be creating an environment where their contributions are valued—and potentially valued even more than yours."

"For people who have only seen it done one way," she continues, "where the loudest voice in the room wins, essentially, and the way you absorb power is by being loud and taking up space. If your goal is to have a learn-it-all culture, you actually can't take [all the] space. Your job [is] to make room for everyone else on your team; and that takes an incredible amount of courage."

Fight and Unite

The key to bringing diverse voices together is to be willing to have the debate and then seek to unify the group with a common goal built on mutual respect and understanding. Management professor and author Morten Hansen writes that teams are best when they "fight and unite."[16] To do this, you must make it safe for others to challenge ideas or assert their point of view. It's impossible to create a free exchange of ideas if people feel intimidated to speak up or challenge conventional wisdom. Rigorous debate can be uncomfortable, but it's necessary. Where debates break down is when they turn toxic or personal. That's why finding unity is so crucial. A team must have the debate, give equal time for everyone to express their view, and, most important, all agree to commit to supporting the outcome.

At Amazon, one of its core cultural principles is to "disagree and commit." Low-level employees are encouraged to make major contributions, and having a high status at the company doesn't prevent you from receiving criticism on your ideas.[17] After a decision is made at Amazon, employees are expected to dedicate themselves fully to it. Essentially, there's a time for a debate and a time for action. That's a "fight and unite" mentality.

By actively asking quieter employees for their opinions or including people with different job functions or life experiences, you'll create an atmosphere in which people feel respected and included. They'll also be much more likely to buy into the culture you're trying to build and unify with others behind your efforts. You'll build advocates, not quiet dissenters. Most important, your culture will reflect the experience and wisdom of many, not just a few.

These behaviors might take more time and patience, but the outcomes are worth it. Culture cannot be mandated. It must be something that you grow together.

Zero Distance

Let me close this chapter by returning to our visit with Satya Nadella.

When he came to visit us in DevDiv, I was beside myself with excitement and nervousness. When he entered our culture room, my pulse began racing, and my brain was screaming, *"There he is! There he is! There he is!"*

Followed by a small entourage, he walked up to each of us, shook our hand, and offered a warm smile. His kind demeanor and gentle nature put all of us at ease.

Monty walked him through the six culture hacks we had applied that influenced and scaled customer obsession in DevDiv (i.e., the next six chapters of this book).

Jessica showed him the HPF and talked about how our teams use the process to engage customers and collect feedback. It was fascinating to see how quickly he understood it and began to apply it. At times, he became animated, walking from one side of the poster to the other to explore new ways that we could utilize the framework.

---

16 [Hansen] pp. 140–165

17 [Sunstein]

I had the opportunity to discuss our workshops, and Satya asked if he could attend, but his assistant was quick to remind him that he didn't have four days available in his schedule. He seemed a bit disappointed with his congested calendar, and I found it amusing that, even as a busy CEO, a chance to learn a new set of skills was still an exciting opportunity for him.

Kelly Krout, a principal UX research manager on our team, then walked with Satya to the center of our lab. From that vantage point, he could see the handful of separate rooms where we were conducting studies with real customers. Our team was on one side of a two-way mirror, with our customers sitting on the other side.

At one point he asked, "Can I go into one of these?" pointing to one of the rooms that was conducting a study with two developers using Visual Studio.

Kelly looked at him a bit incredulously. I'm sure he was thinking, *"You're the CEO, you can go anywhere you want!"*

From behind the glass, he stood with the product team and watched our customers use Visual Studio in real time. His smile was wide as he leaned in to get a closer look. After acknowledging several of the product team members conducting the study, he asked Kelly, "So is everyone here a researcher?"

Kelly replied, "No," and started pointing to each person in the room: "In this study, we have a program manager, an engineer, a technical writer, and a designer." He then pointed to Karl Melder, a researcher on our team who was standing in the back corner of the tiny lab room. "That's Karl. He's our researcher; he's organized the study. The team benefits by interacting with the customer directly, so he likes to get out of the way, this way they have a direct connection with the customer. In this case, our program manager is asking the questions during this interview."

Like many large companies, Microsoft has also struggled with its top-down structure and strict adherence to job titles and descriptions. It's not uncommon to see fiefdoms sprout where practitioners safeguard their functions to protect their jobs.

What Satya saw in our lab, was that Karl was glad to take a backseat and have a program manager play the role of researcher. Our goal in DevDiv is to put zero distance between product teams and our customers. That's what we obsess over. In this example, Karl was following through on Satya's mission by helping his *colleagues* achieve more.

This was Satya's vision for the company culture, a highly collaborative group who invested in each other to best learn from and serve the customer.

In his book *Hit Refresh*, Satya reflected on his visit to DevDiv:

It is refreshing to see how they have rewired their own product creation process to be more focused on customers—exploring hypotheses and then validating or disproving them through testing and engagement with people who buy and use our technologies and services. The logic was to change their language to open themselves to possibilities.[18]

Without Satya's clear mission and the tireless work of so many others to reform the attitudes and behaviors of people at the company, DevDiv's transformation wouldn't have been possible.

The foundation had been put in place; the Priority Zero cultural elements were being addressed. The rest was up to us, just as it's now up to you.

With that in mind, let's dig into our first culture hack.

---

18 [Nadella] p. 245

2

Establish a Common Language

Famed linguist and pioneer Benjamin Whorf once wrote that "language shapes the way we think, and determines what we think about."[1] Essentially, what we talk about and how we talk about it reflects our reality.

Now, the controversies over "linguistic determinism" are well beyond the scope of this book, but we should recognize that the words we use matter.

This has been the case with our journey in DevDiv. We found that when our leaders and product team members communicated using a common language, it was a powerful way to not only collaborate, but to connect ourselves to one another and our customers. Introducing a new way to talk about what we were doing and share the progress of our learnings was a powerful tool in developing our customer-driven culture.

It's with that in mind that we share this first important hack.

How Language Binds Us Together

In the summer of 2007, Chris Messina, a product designer living in San Francisco, was frustrated. He was having trouble following along with a conversation happening on Twitter about Barcamp, a Silicon Valley meetup of entrepreneurs and tech geniuses. The messages and profiles were scattered all over the website, and there was no way to see all the conversations regarding the conference in one place.

He tweeted a modest proposal:

How do you feel about using # (pound) for groups. As in #barcamp [msg]?

---

1 [Whorf] p. 5

Stowe Boyd, an anthropologist studying the future of work, tweeted support a couple days later:

I support the hash tag convention.

And as simply as that, the notion of a hashtag on Twitter was born. It ushered in an entirely new way to communicate and connect with others online.

However, Twitter wasn't convinced. Messina later told *The Wall Street Journal,* "[Twitter] told me flat out, 'These things are for nerds. They're never going to catch on.'"[2] Messina even went to Twitter headquarters to pitch the idea of using hashtags to cofounder Biz Stone. According to Messina, his reply was curt: "No. But thanks for your enthusiasm."

What Twitter couldn't have predicted was that the hashtag would become an incredibly useful mechanism for its users to organize themselves.

During the San Diego fires of 2007, Twitter hashtag usage reached critical mass as users tagged their latest updates with #sandiegofire.[3] This created a level of citizen journalism never before seen online. What users discovered was that they could get nearly instant information from a wide gamut of perspectives during a crisis. For better or worse, the public now had access to near-instant information when a tragedy or disaster hit.

Eventually, Twitter embraced the hashtag, turning them into links that, when clicked, provided a view of only messages marked with that hashtag. They even added a guide to their website instructing users how to best formulate a hashtag for their tweets.

When we look at this phenomenon a little more closely, we can appreciate that there's something much more powerful at play than the simple organization of tweets. Today, a hashtag can go viral and become a shortcut for people to join a shared idea or identity. Entire social movements have been organized and executed just by using a hashtag. This collective behavior of hashtags illustrates the power of having a common language.

Therefore, your organizational culture cannot gain traction and flourish if it doesn't have the appropriate, common language. Essentially, as illustrated in Figure 2-1, if you change the language, it will start to change the thinking. This change in thinking will change the actions of your employees and eventually change the entire value system and culture of your organization.

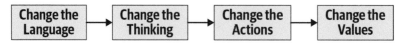

Figure 2-1. Changing your language ultimately changes your values and your culture

---

2 [Zak]

3 [Bigelow]

So the question becomes: "If we must drive culture by pursuing a common language, what should that language be?"

Change the Language

It turns out that the basic scientific method gives us the best language to encourage a learning mindset. This means that you shift from a language that supports what you know and focus your attention on the things you still need to learn. We want to identify our assumptions, formulate them into hypotheses, and run experiments to validate or invalidate our thinking. These words help us remain in a constant state of learning while amassing confidence in our existing knowledge over time.

With our product teams, we use *The Customer-Driven Playbook* and our workshops to train them in the process of formulating their assumptions into testable hypotheses. Capturing our assumptions about the customer and their problems is a powerful exercise for any product team.

Essentially, we want teams to fall into a cadence in which they're continually evaluating their assumptions against what they're learning from our customers. We call it our *customer-driven cadence*, and it's an ever-revolving cycle of assumptions, hypotheses, experiments, and sense-making, as depicted in Figure 2-2. For DevDiv, this language of learning—assumptions, hypotheses, experiments, and sense-making—comprises powerful words that make up our cadence of software development.

Figure 2-2. DevDiv's customer-driven cadence and language of learning: assumptions, hypotheses, experiments, and sense-making

The words we use shape our outlook. When we say, "I have a hypothesis," instead of saying, "I know our customers want this feature," we open ourselves to the fact that we could be wrong about our assumptions. Moving to a language of learning and experimentation can be liberating because it makes it *OK* to be wrong.

However, the business world often doesn't afford us this luxury. People are paid to be correct and, in the technology industry, we often lavish praise on the "rebel genius" who was spot on when everyone else was wrong. Those stories are plentiful and well covered in the press.

What's often overlooked are the myriad failures that tech luminaries like Steve Jobs, Bill Gates, and Jeff Bezos experienced on their journeys to becoming legends.

Before Steve Jobs changed the world with his iPod and iPhone, he was behind consumer flops like the Newton and the NeXT Cube. Famed innovator and CEO of Tesla and SpaceX, Elon Musk, once applied for a job at Netscape and never got a reply, even after hanging out in their lobby.[4]

When the focus of your work is to experiment with your assumptions, it becomes a quest for answers—not a quest to prove yourself right. A language of learning takes the ego out of it, leaving a pursuit of knowledge in its wake. That can be liberating, particularly in an atmosphere like Microsoft (and so many other companies), where a pursuit of one's own personal achievement can reign supreme.

Stating that you have an assumption about a customer's motivation or behavior puts that belief in the proper context and frees it from a sense of ownership, releasing the fear that comes with finding out that your assumption was wrong. In fact, in DevDiv, we almost *delight* in being proven wrong because, like Edison, we've discovered another way it won't work. The important point here is that assumptions aren't a bad thing. They're a mental shortcut that reveals ideas based on previous experience or observations. The problem with assumptions is when they remain untested. If we're not careful, untested assumptions quickly become untested "facts."

Therefore, in DevDiv, you'll find that words like assumption, hypothesis, and experiment are part of our daily lingua franca. It wasn't always this way, but through purposeful encouragement and modeling, it evolved in that direction. These terms were introduced in communications from leadership, reinforced in product reviews, and taught in our workshops. We had to invoke them wherever appropriate to create an atmosphere in which employees were hearing these terms multiple times each day.

Much like a viral Twitter hashtag, this language of learning became a visible way to show that you were part of the culture of DevDiv. The language became a social norm, and you were considered an outsider if you were unwilling to approach new product ideas with a learning-first, customer-driven mindset. Basically, to show that you belonged to the new movement that put customers at the center of everything we were doing, you needed to use the language of learning.

Use Language to Change the Thinking

It's critically important that the language you choose is accessible by everyone. In DevDiv, nearly half of the employees are engineers. Even though the UX researcher, designer, and

---

4 [Clifford]

program manager were often seen as the people responsible for customer development, we knew that for everyone to share in the journey, we needed a language that would make sense to our engineers as well. Fortunately, the language of learning (assumptions, hypotheses, experiments, and sense-making) were terms that were being celebrated in the Lean software movement. These were Agile methods our engineers were already adopting and integrating into their development work. Our engineers already wanted to adopt Lean methods, and books from authors like Eric Ries, who wrote the immensely popular book *The Lean Startup*, were showing up in team rooms and engineering meetings.

The Lean movement was built upon an ethos of rapid learning and experimentation, using words like "assumptions," "hypotheses," and "experiment." By reinforcing these words in our culture, we were able to exploit the excitement our product teams already had about the Lean movement. These terms provided a common ground where engineers, program managers, researchers, and designers could come together and evaluate their work.

Encouraging the use of hypotheses empowered our teams to track and share what they were learning and became an essential part of promoting our language of learning.

Many of us learned to write hypotheses in our high school science class, but we still found that teams struggled to produce hypotheses that could be used in meaningful ways. Many of them were just vague statements that could be applied to just about any customer segment or problem.

For example, it wasn't uncommon to see hypotheses that targeted generic customer segments, like, "We believe that *developers* are…" If you're at all familiar with the developer space, you know that there are *hundreds* of types of developers. You have enterprise developers, small business developers, consultants, hobbyists, desktop, web, mobile, Internet of Things (IoT), just to name a few.

When the team's hypotheses targeted literally everyone in our customer base, it created difficulty because they made their way through the customer-driven cadence. They were ending up with generic learnings that weren't helpful or targeted. It became a sort of "garbage in, garbage out" problem. Although writing hypotheses might have been what some Americans learn in eighth grade, studies show that nearly half of Americans have trouble identifying a proper hypothesis and understanding the entire scientific process.[5] In other words, we found that writing testable hypotheses wasn't something that just came naturally to people.

That's what inspired us to create the HPF, which we discussed in Preface. It became a vital tool because it included a set of templates to make it easy for teams to formulate their hypotheses. Each stage had its own template (e.g., Customer, Problem, Concept, Feature, and Business). Depending on where the team was in its development life cycle, it could choose the appropriate stage and create a fully formed hypothesis, as shown in Figure 2-3.

---

5 [Kennedy]

Customer Development

Customer

We believe [type of customers] are motivated to [motivation] when doing [job-to-be-done]

Problem

We believe [type of customers] are frustrated by [job-to-be-done] because of [problem]

Figure 2-3. Hypothesis templates for the first two stages of the HPF (Customer and Problem stages)

Frameworks like the HPF proved invaluable in creating an instruction set for working with our new language. All our product teams had to do was fill in the template with their assumptions, and they would have a fully formed hypothesis, ready for testing.

When building your cultural language, we highly advocate employing hypotheses as a key instrument to root your language in learning. You'll quickly find that everyone has the capacity to create them. You can even use them to engage your detractors. Many of them will have their own opinions of how you should proceed with culture change. Having them express those ideas as hypotheses will not only get them practicing your language of learning, but it will also help them realize that their suggestions are based on their own assumptions. It involves them in the discussion in a way that puts them in a learning mindset, even when they're disagreeing with you.

If you create an environment in which teams are trading and evaluating their hypotheses, you create a culture that is dependent on learning. As product teams engage with and learn from their customers, you'll find that they'll respond more quickly to customer demands because when an idea has been proven wrong, they won't waste time protecting their egos; they'll just update their hypotheses, iterate on their idea, and keep learning.

Use Language to Change the Actions

Moving to a common language takes practice. It's like a new pair of shoes: they feel a bit awkward at first, but as soon as you break them in, they feel like an extension of your feet.

One of the most profound changes we saw was when leaders began to model our language of learning.

During our engineering reviews, our corporate vice president, Julia Liuson, would ask questions like, "What is your hypothesis about this customer?" and, "What are your assumptions about the customer's problem?"

This was a subtle change in language, but it proved to be overwhelmingly effective. Teams realized that, to get through a successful engineering review, they would need to identify the assumptions that had led them to their decisions. After those assumptions were identified, teams needed a way to communicate them to our leadership team and one another and demonstrate how they had collected data from customers to validate or invalidate their thinking.

The structure of the hypothesis fit the bill. Soon, teams were leading engineering reviews with Excel spreadsheets full of hypotheses. Others had them written down in OneNote, Microsoft Word, or email. Some teams began to tag their hypotheses as "validated," "invalidated," and "inconclusive."

The method didn't really matter. What was more important was that our leadership team could easily follow along with a team's progress, and the entire review process was led not by anyone's opinions, but by everyone's desire to update their learning.

Teams also adopted Lean experimentation methods for validating or invalidating their hypotheses. Teams began to engage in "Quick Pulse" studies in which they would share iterations of product ideas with customers—to validate or invalidate their assumptions—every week. The game of product making in DevDiv had shifted from "How can I convince everyone that I'm right?" to "How quickly can I learn if I'm wrong?"

Each year, our teams in DevDiv have more than 10,000 direct customer interactions, whether by directly observing customer behavior or directly talking to customers.

These actions occur because we now have a culture that is obsessed with learning and experimenting. Continually refining our assumptions with our customers proves to be a fruitful landscape for exploring ideas and learning quickly.

Use Language to Change the Values

When an organization begins to adopt new activities and behaviors such as a language of learning, new values also begin to emerge. Effectively, the moment that DevDiv shifted to an organization that was motivated to learn, we began to value the work teams spent learning from their customers.

We began to identify innovations, not just in our product features, but in how we could put zero distance between us and our customers. Teams were getting creative with how they connected with customers because it became clear to everyone that customer connections were the new currency.

For example, many of our program managers were using developer conferences and local meetups as an opportunity to grow their customer network. Others were using sites like LinkedIn, Twitter, and Reddit to find new customers to talk with. There was also a huge demand for our UX research team to guide and mentor our product teams in interviewing techniques and customer development strategies. It turned out that our product teams had a deep desire to create better connections with their customers; they just needed tools, like the HPF, that provided a pathway to do it effectively.

Your organizational values stem from what you talk about and what you give attention to. Therefore, your language, thinking, and actions are an expression of your values. In DevDiv, our values evolved from being celebrated for reaching a shipping milestone to being celebrated for connecting with customers to learn.

Consider a Language of Positivity

When working toward a customer-driven culture, it's easy to get into the mindset of focusing on what isn't working. Too often, we fall victim to obsessing over every individual who is resisting change. We lament that they're unwilling to incorporate customer feedback into their decision making or, even worse, think they know the customer better than anyone else in the organization. Sometimes, they sabotage our efforts or are vocally resistant to our proposals.

These "problem children" get the most attention because we see them as the ultimate obstacle to conquer in order to achieve our ultimate goals. We obsess over them, strategize about them, and convince ourselves we've failed because they haven't come over to our way of thinking. We say to ourselves, "If we can just win them over, everyone else will fall in line."

Focusing on where you're weakest or vulnerable is important, but it shouldn't be the only signal you're considering as you experiment with various methods to build your culture. With all the hyperattention given to what isn't working, we run the risk of missing key situations where we've made progress, making it more difficult to repeat that success.

In the late 1980s, management and organizational literature was dominated with problem-solving techniques. Their focus was to understand and frame problems so that they could be efficiently analyzed and corrected. Although dealing with problems is a key management function, it also created a language that focused energy on everything that was going wrong.

In the book *Management and Organization: Relational Alternatives to Individualism*, the authors propose that "language is the vehicle that makes knowing possible by describing or picturing the objectivities of 'that-which-is.'"[6] Therefore, words we use to describe our circumstance affect our mindset, our strategy, and our outcome. Put another way, if we're constantly talking about our problems, we don't give ourselves enough time to talk about potential solutions.

Appreciative inquiry is a style of change management that encourages us to ask more questions about what is working rather than what is not. The goal of appreciative inquiry isn't to delude ourselves into believing everything is fine; it's to help us investigate and learn from situations that have had a positive outcome.

---

6 [Cooperrider]

Agents of Change: Monique and Jerry Sternin

To illustrate this idea, consider the story of Monique and Jerry Sternin. As staff members of Save the Children, a nonprofit organization founded in the early 1900s, they shared a mission of giving all children a healthy start in life. In 1990, their work brought them to Vietnam, where nearly half of the country's children were malnourished.

When they arrived with their 10-year-old son, they found themselves completely out of their depth. They didn't speak the language, they had a minimal staff, and even fewer resources. "We were like orphans at the airport," Jerry recalls. "We had no idea what we were going to do."[7]

Additionally, the Vietnamese government wasn't entirely supportive. The small team was given six months to produce results. If they couldn't, they would be expected to leave.

As the Sternins saw it, the way nonprofits like Save the Children were dealing with malnutrition was not entirely effective. They would go into underdeveloped areas, teach the inhabitants about the importance of good sanitation, protecting their water supply, and the benefits of an organized food distribution plan. However, the moment they went back home, all their hard work would be reversed as villagers crept back to their old ways. Additionally, six months was not enough time to set up those types of infrastructures. The villagers were leery of outsiders and were frustrated by previous attempts that had failed. From their baseline assessments, the Sternins could see that 64% of the children in villages they planned to target were at risk of starvation.[8] These children were dying. The team would need to hit the ground running and think quickly.

Instead of wasting time getting an understanding of every problem that was contributing to the crisis, they decided to employ appreciative inquiry. They would go into their targeted villages and talk with families whose children were *not* malnourished. In Dan and Chip Heath's book *Switch: How to Change Things When Change is Hard*, they refer to this method as "finding the bright spots."[9] Essentially, the Sternins and their team would focus on the bright-spot families to help them illuminate ways to help the families that were struggling.

For example, bright-spot families were feeding their healthy kids more frequently throughout the day. Technically, it was the same amount of food as struggling families, but instead of feeding them two large meals each day, they were feeding them four smaller meals. These smaller amounts were easier for the children to digest and gave their bodies time to absorb the nutrients.

---

7 [Dorsey]
8 [Dyer] p. 68
9 [Heath] p. 27

Another finding was how the bright-spot families ate. Struggling families assumed that smaller children could take care of themselves, believing that they would feed themselves when they were hungry. Bright-spot families would hand-feed their children if necessary.

Armed with these insights, the team created a program in which 50 struggling families would meet daily at a hut and prepare food. During these meetings, they shared their findings and trained families with skills of basic food cleanliness and preparation. The families used this time to discuss what was working and to get advice on how to improve their techniques. This focused ritual of food preparation became the norm, and families began to develop their own knowledge networks to help one another and their children thrive.

Six months after arriving in Vietnam, 65% of the children in the study were measurably more nourished and, most important, they were staying that way.

There are many lessons that we can learn from this story of culture change, but what's most exciting about the Sternin's story is the power of a positive mindset. The Sternins could've easily arrived in Vietnam, outnumbered and unwelcomed, and thrown up their hands, saying, "These people don't want our help!" They could've faced the impossible six-month window and said, "This can't be done, we will need much more time." Instead of spending the entire six months cataloging all the various problems that were leading to the malnourishment of children, they decided to focus on what was working well and try to repeat it in the areas that needed the most help.

Consider this in your own cultural movement:

- Are you spending enough time examining when things move in the correct direction?
- What can we learn from those situations and, more important, can it be repeated elsewhere in the organization?

It's not that you should ignore your problem areas; it's that those areas are not always the best place to find your next innovative idea. Think about spreading your analysis of your cultural efforts. Dive deep into areas where you've made progress and develop new hypotheses that can be carried to more difficult parts of your organization.

Many times, our past successes provide answers for our future challenges.

Additionally, positive language can be more motivating. If you're in a situation in which morale is low or the team is frustrated with poor outcomes, perhaps shifting the focus to what is going well can be the approach that helps your culture team uncover new insights.

In her book *The Influential Mind: What the Brain Reveals About Our Power to Change Others*, author Tali Sharot says:

*When we are stressed, we become fixated on detecting dangers; we focus on what can
go wrong. This then creates excessively pessimistic views, which, in turn, can cause us
to become overly conservative.[10]*

It's really no different when we experience organizational change. For many, this change
can cause stress because you might need to adopt new behaviors and learn new skills. In these
moments, it's all too easy to point to everything that isn't working as evidence that the organization is moving in the wrong direction.

Use the Hypotheses for Exploring Cultural Initiatives

As we saw our language of learning evolve in concert with the HPF, it became clear that we
could absolutely shape our culture with the same experimental mindset that we were applying
to build our products. The language of learning—assumptions, hypotheses, experiments—
proved to be the perfect set of tools to experiment with cultural changes as well.

An example of this was an initiative we started in DevDiv called Culture Club. Every year,
Microsoft conducts an "MS Poll," which is a survey given to all employees to determine where
we are on things like the Work-Health Index (WHI) and Leadership Index (LI). Essentially, it's
a way for all employees to give feedback on things like the effectiveness of our leaders, their
work/life balance, and feelings on where the company is headed.

One area for which we received feedback was the challenge in preparing managers for
leadership. We needed to make people management more accessible to employees and give
them opportunities to explore whether people management was right for them.

In late 2017, Ryan Salva, Julia Liuson's chief of staff, was tasked with improving these metrics and to invest in building the next generation of qualified leaders.

"From the management side of things," Ryan explains, "our directors were facing a deficit
of qualified candidates for people managers. They were running out of leads and they were
searching for ways to increase the strength of their leads bench."[11]

Additionally, senior-level employees were asking Ryan for advice on how to get into people
management:

*We had a senior-level [employee] who was thinking about pursuing people manage-
ment, but he didn't know how one gets into it; and even then, he didn't know if people
management was right for him, because the only example he had to follow was watching his own manager.*

---

10 [Sharot] p. 136
11 [Salva]

Ryan saw this as an opportunity to do some experimentation and solve two pressing problems: the need to invest in building the next group of talented leaders and the need for new voices and faces to emerge as leaders in DevDiv. Ryan partnered with a couple of enterprising employees (who were also interested in getting into people management), and together they crafted some hypotheses using the HPF (see Figure 2-4). They used the framework because it had become familiar to them during their product development. Even though this project represented a cultural initiative rather than a product or feature, they still saw that they could use the framework to identify their assumptions.

Customer Development

Customer	Problem
We believe [senior-level employees] **are motivated to** [learn if people management is right for them] **when** [exploring career advancement opportunities]	We believe [senior-level employees] **are frustrated when** [exploring career advancement opportunities] **because of [the lack of information around people management]**

Figure 2-4. How Ryan and his team used the HPF to explore Customer and Problem hypotheses

Essentially, Ryan and his team had a Customer and Problem hypothesis. In this case, their customers were their fellow coworkers:

Type of customers
Senior-level employees

Motivation
Learn whether people management is right for them

Job-to-be-done
Exploring options to advance their career

Problem
The lack of information on how to get into people management

After completing a handful of interviews with their peers, the team came up with an idea for a manager panel discussion. This would be an opportunity for managers to present topics and answer questions surrounding the role and responsibilities of people management. It could be an open and supportive dialog in which employees and managers (from diverse experiences and backgrounds) could discuss and shape what people management *should* be for our organization.

Again, they used the Concept hypothesis template from the HPF to formulate the idea, as demonstrated in Figure 2-5.

Product Development

Concept

We believe a [manager panel discussion] will solve [the lack of information around people management] when [exploring career advancement opportunities]

Figure 2-5. The Concept stage of the HPF includes a hypothesis template for exploring concepts like a manager panel discussion

The point here is not to unpack the entirety of the HPF (that's covered extensively in *The Customer-Driven Playbook*); rather, it's to appreciate how hypotheses and a language of learning can be applied to cultural initiatives, just like they are applied to product initiatives.

In this case, Ryan and the team theorized that a manager panel discussion would be the best way to address the lack of information available to employees exploring career opportunities in management. Just like a new feature in a product, there could've been many ways for the team to address this problem. The panel discussion was only one idea of many, so it needed to be tested to determine whether employees found the solution valuable.

"We started an experiment by having a single panel discussion," Ryan says. "It was a 20-minute presentation by an experienced manager on what it means to be a manager, followed by a Q+A....We were thinking, you know, maybe we'll get one to two dozen folks to attend. The first panel discussion had over 115 people show up," Ryan remembers.

This was a very strong signal that they had landed on a valuable concept, so the team decided to invest further.

They've since created the Aspiring Managers Series, which is a series of similar panel discussions designed to help employees chart their careers into management. They've found that this not only removes the mysticism on what's required to become a lead in DevDiv, but it also gives all employees a better understanding of how their managers can help them shape their careers. It's created an avenue for leaders and employees to get together and learn from one another about what makes a great people manager.

The team continues to evolve its understanding by formulating its hypotheses and experimenting with various programs. Each time, they make iterations based on qualitative feedback (e.g., interviewing employees) and quantitative data (e.g., surveys and attendance records).

This is the same pattern DevDiv uses when building and shaping products for customers. In this case, the Aspiring Managers Series is the product, and its target customers are senior-level employees trying to advance their careers. Attendance and employee feedback will shape the series going forward, and the Culture Club team will take those learnings and apply them to other programs designed to promote diversity and inclusion.

This is an incredible example of the power of the three vital behaviors of change (awareness, curiosity, and courage). The team was aware that there were gaps in the leadership bench and were curious to see whether there was a desire among staff to receive leadership training. Finally, they had the courage to try something different—running a panel discussion to test the waters and see how much interest there was before investing in a huge, overly funded initiative.

Be Mindful of Everyday Language

Language is one of the most valuable tools that will affect the culture of your organization. Therefore, you must be mindful of your day-to-day operating language. It must be a language of action that can be used in everyday situations, and it should be reinforced in all communications from the board room to the team room.

Disney refers to Disneyland park attendees as "guests" and its staff as "cast members." This language is intentional, and it reminds employees that their core focus is to create a larger-than-life experience for the thousands of families that arrive at the park each day. Starbucks calls their employees "partners" to reinforce that all employees have a vested interest in the success of the company. This is also supported by the fact that all Starbucks employees receive stock in the company based on the amount of time they've worked there. These language choices are intentional and have deep meaning within their respective organizations. The language your organization or team uses becomes a shared identity on which you operate. It tells newcomers, "This is what we value, because this is how we chose to name things."

In the case of DevDiv, we value a culture where employees are connected and learning from our customers. To do that, we reinforce a language of learning using hypotheses, experiments, and the HPF. In turn, we take advantage of those very same mechanisms to experiment with various cultural initiatives.

Therefore, you should consider the language that your organization is using every day and determine whether it aligns to a culture that is driven by your customers. Are you asking employees to "create amazing customer experiences," but your day-to-day language is full of how to "optimize customer revenue"? Are you asking employees to "have greater customer empathy," yet the language in your meetings is full of emotionless usage metrics or adoption numbers?

In their book *Organizational Culture and Leadership*, authors Edgar and Peter Schein sum it up perfectly:

> *As a group grows, has success, and develops an identity, the shared learning process broadens from just the minimum behavior we need to agree on to get the job done to a language, a way to think, and a way to feel.*[12]

That's what your organizational language provides. It's a roadmap for employees to understand a way to think and a way to feel.

We included a list of useful maxims in the back of this book. These maxims can be helpful in creating short, punchy, and memorable sayings that can spread virally within your teams and organization.

Applying the Hack

Here are steps that you can take to hack the language of your organization to be more customer driven:

- As you begin to build your own language of learning for your organization, you might consider how to employ terms that have worked well in DevDiv's customer-driven transformation. Terms like "assumption," "experiment," and "hypothesis" are great starting points.

- As your language evolves, you might consider other terms that we've found to be successful in building a language of learning: "customer motivation," "customer 'jobs-to-be-done,'" "problems," "concepts," "unique value proposition," "business outcome," "validation/invalidation," "inconclusive findings." You can start to sprinkle these terms in your communications, publications, and presentations.

---

12 [Schein]

- Provide your team a "glossary of terms" so that they can see the proposed language and align to it. At first, trying to change old habits (especially ways of speaking) can feel forced and awkward. If necessary, gently suggest the preferred language, in a fun and positive way.

- Ask new questions in your product or engineering reviews, such as:

  — Who is the customer you're serving?

  — What is their motivation?

  — What problem does this solution solve for them?

  — How impactful is this problem for them?

  — How confident are you that this solution solves the problem?

  Questions like these will encourage reflection and learning. They tie the decisions that are being made in the product to direct customer needs.

- Maintain a backlog of assumptions, hypotheses, and planned experiments. You want to track these things over time to see the evolution of your learning as a team.

- Create a consistent and easy-to-read template for sharing your hypotheses. For example, you might create an email template that has a table to track your assumptions or hypotheses. Columns in the table might include: the type of hypotheses (customer, problem, concept, feature, or business) and the status (invalidated, confirmed, or inconclusive).

- Help managers and leaders by reviewing emails, presentations, videos, and any other publications. Look for opportunities to showcase your key terms to reinforce the language of learning as a strong belonging cue.

- Work with your product teams *before* product reviews with leadership. Review presentations and encourage the use of the key terms. You can also help them prepare by role playing and assuming the role of someone from the leadership team. You can ask them questions like, "Who is the customer?" "What problem are you trying to solve?" and, "What makes you confident that this is the right problem to solve?" As they practice their answers, you can give them feedback to help them identify the weak spots in their arguments that can be supported with richer customer data.

3

Build Bridges, Not Walls

When you closely examine the story of any breakthrough innovation, you're likely to find that it was built on the accumulated knowledge from work that preceded it. Certainly, brilliant innovators deserve their rightful place in history. But we seem to always forget that their contributions to society were often nurtured within potent learning networks.

Another powerful hack we've come across in our cultural transformation is when groups are willing to share learnings across team and divisional boundaries. This might seem like an obvious idea, but we often don't account for just how difficult it can be to share your expertise in highly competitive environments. In a sense, giving away what makes you special is viewed as a sure-fire way to make yourself obsolete. Every company wants cross-functional and highly collaborative teams, but tensions arise when people choose to focus only on work that will help them advance their own personal goals and professional aspirations.

Each time you watch a colleague get credit for an idea you inspired or a director get promoted for a successful team project, feelings of animosity or even contempt will naturally arise. Many of us are willing to collaborate so long as our original impact is clearly identified and acknowledged. However, that's nearly impossible because collaboration is fast and messy. Ideas can be generated, discarded, and completely restructured all in a matter of a single discussion.

We should be fearless champions of our own work. After all, there's no better person to explain the benefits of what you contribute to your organization than you. However, we must also acknowledge that credit-seeking and gatekeeping can be toxic and can have severe ramifications on the overall output of your team.

In this chapter, we explore how building bridges of knowledge and tearing down silos of expertise is a vital component of any cultural transformation. The sharing of knowledge, freely and openly, is foundational to a learning-first organization.

Giving Away Your Expertise

Building the very best software in an increasingly competitive world is challenging. We have software teams that find themselves in direct competition with one another all the time. It's the nature of generating ideas and building on the work of others.

Some of you might remember the comical "org chart" that still circulates on the internet today, which you can see in Figure 3-1. It depicts Microsoft's internal orgs in a standoff, guns drawn and pointing at one another.

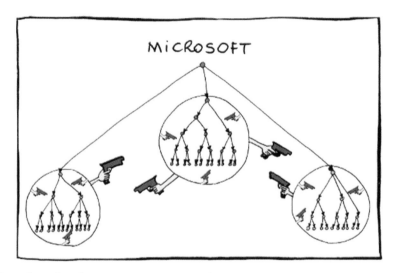

Figure 3-1. Microsoft org chart from Manu Cornet's "Org Charts" comic

Although my personal experience over the past six years suggests that we've made a lot of positive progress in this area, it wasn't that long ago that Microsoft's reputation was that of a company full of siloed "fiefdoms" and infighting.

When Satya sent the call for the company to strive for greater customer empathy and connection, our own research team had to come to grips with the fact that user research and customer development would be skills that were expected by many other disciplines at Microsoft.

Satya's call was for *all* of us to be invested in learning from the customer, not just the user researchers.

In DevDiv, our product teams rose to the challenge with newfound enthusiasm and energy. They wanted to be empowered with the ability to do their own customer research. Product managers, engineers, and designers were asking for help with interviewing techniques and for feedback on their discussion guides. They were recruiting their own customers and building their own customer councils to help them shape product decisions. They were generating their own customer evidence and presenting findings that informed our leadership about emerging customer behaviors and consumer trends. One of the most challenging aspects about all of this was that they were getting good at it! To be honest, this was a bit of a scary proposition. It seemed as if our unique skills as user researchers were being "outsourced" to the rest of the company. Many of us had dedicated our careers and spent a lot of money on education to excel in the area of user research.

It would've seemed completely reasonable to dig in our heels—to put up walls—and immediately step in to gatekeep progress. We could've gone into our product team rooms like resident advisors conducting dorm-room searches: "OK everyone, put that hypothesis down! That needs an expert review before you test it with a customer!" We could have rung alarm bells and frightened our leadership into thinking our product teams weren't ready to do the level of research that we were capable of. We could've focused all our attention on finding stories of teams doing research "wrong" and elevated these situations as examples of why the division needed us now more than ever.

Fortunately, Monty had a different vision for our team: one that positioned us as coaches, giving away our expertise to empower an army of product people to learn about our customers. This wasn't a selfless or altruistic act. It was a matter of necessity. The train had left the station, and our teams were conducting Lean experimentation and customer development at an exponential rate. We could choose to step in front of that train and try to stop it, or we could hop on and help steer it in the proper direction. Additionally, we saw this as an incredible opportunity to help scale the efforts of a small research team. If everyone was investing in learning from our customers, our ability to raise the organization's IQ about the customer and their needs was exponential.

Who Owns the Voice of the Customer?

As you pursue an organization that strives for zero distance between product makers and their customers, you might encounter pushback from disciplines that see themselves as responsible for collecting and reporting on customer insights. These experts, from user research, customer support, data science, marketing, quality control, product management, or design, might feel threatened, as if the work they do is being democratized.

The reality is that no one owns the voice of the customer except for the customer themselves. In a customer-driven organization, everyone must be responsible for connecting with customers and learning from them.

During the Mind the Product conference in San Francisco, Tricia Wang, a Fellow at the Berkman Center at Harvard University and cofounder of Sudden Compass, a consultancy that helps enterprises with customer development, discussed the role of user researchers in this emerging landscape where customer learning is becoming democratized. In her keynote address, she said:

In a cross-functional world, researchers move from being methodology gurus to discovery guides. Researchers don't deliver the voice of the customer; researchers enable everyone to speak and to hear the voice of the customer. Your job is no longer the executioner of research, but about embedding yourself in the business as partners. To enable everyone to experience the customer and to facilitate that cross-functional conversation about that experience; to best impact product.[1]

As a research team, we came to the same conclusion. We found tremendous value in empowering our product teams to connect with and learn from customers. In fact, we were seeing that our organization valued our role as researchers even more, challenging us to find innovative ways to share our skills with all nonresearchers in DevDiv. Our role had evolved from being a small team that learned on behalf of the many to a team that would empower everyone to learn.

In the game of interoffice politics, having expert knowledge or desirable resources can be valuable. In unhealthy cultures, company experts can become gatekeepers, holding onto information or doling it out slowly to control the way the information is shared or evaluated. The motivations can be many, but often this need to control information stems from a desire to safeguard their role or function. The thinking goes, "They'll never get rid of us, we're the only ones who know how to..."

As your company transitions to a customer-obsessed culture, you might find those disciplines (UX, user research, design, customer support, marketing, data science, product management, etc.) begin to act as gatekeepers, trying to control the dissemination of skills and learning. It can be well intentioned and necessary; some might cite the dangers of letting employees talk directly with customers or suggest the harm that can come from sharing early ideas with customers.

It's not that these concerns are without merit. Opening your business and regularly gathering information from customers, even with their consent, is a big responsibility that shouldn't be taken lightly. When customers trust you with their data and their feedback, you're entering an agreement to use that information in a responsible and secure way, and one that benefits them. However, the need to control the data that's being collected, if left unchecked, can put more distance between product makers and their customers than is necessary. Taking a stance against learning and the free and open exchange of ideas is like taking a stance against the sun shining in the sky.

Sometimes, we must look at the bigger picture within our cultural transformation. Sharing knowledge, experience, and expertise is vital in getting an organization to change. For a customer-driven culture to take root, you must maintain that no single team completely owns

---

1 [Tate-Wang]

the customer experience. It must be experienced together so that everyone can participate in the greater goal of delighting customers. Allowing others to adopt duties from your team, especially if you're already responsible for connecting with customers, is a great way to apply your skills in new and more valuable ways. Industries will always require experts, but when you're trying to move your organization to Lean experimentation and customer connection, these experts can get in the way of greater organizational learning and growth.

Consider how you, as a cultural change agent, can encourage others to share their knowledge. Create opportunities where cross-functional teams can learn from one another's disciplines—sharing techniques, customer learnings, and new ways to frame problems.

Sharing Knowledge in DevDiv

It's incredible when we bring a software engineer into our user research lab and allow them to talk directly with customers. At first, they might be nervous, especially when interviewing a customer in front of an "expert user researcher." However, through our encouragement and guidance, we're able to create a powerful moment of customer connection that far outweighs the impact of a 20-page report on customer findings. In those moments, the engineer, designer, or program manager makes a lasting connection with a person who uses their product. There's a sense of ownership and responsibility that comes with that exchange. The customer no longer remains a nameless user or a set of ones and zeros stored in a database.

In fact, we welcome any member of the product team to participate in learning from the customer themselves. We don't want to create distance between them and their customers.

Inspired by Cindy Alvarez's book *Lean Customer Development: Build Products Your Customer Will Buy*, we believe people are primarily motivated by three things:[2]

- They want to feel smart.
- They want to help others.
- They want to fix things.

Viewed through this lens, consider how your cultural changes and training are assisting each discipline to acquire new capabilities.

When we conduct our workshops, coaching employees in the art of customer development, we're mindful that our materials don't come off as if we're the experts—loading the audience with technical jargon and pedantic domain knowledge, or making needling corrections to ensure people feel out of their depth and overwhelmed with all they need to learn to

2 [Alvarez] p. 32

perform their own customer development. That would serve only to reinforce our expertise and (if I were being honest) might even make us feel superior.

It's more important for our tools to be accessible, easy to get started with, and immediately useful.

No matter what your core area of expertise or professional discipline is, spend time looking over your own materials. Do they make people who are digesting them feel smart? Are they easy to use, and, do they give your employees enough knowledge to get started quickly? Or are they full of "do's and don'ts," creating a negative energy that zaps the fun out of creating customer connections? Are you enforcing policies that, when you observe them closely, are in place to protect only a single team's expertise?

Build Great Products by Improving Both Sides of the Glass

There's a powerful moment when a product team comes into our user research lab. They'll sit on one side of the glass (the employee side) and observe the customer through a one-way mirror (the customer side). The customer is aware the team is on the other side of the glass, but not being able to see the team's reaction helps them to focus on the tasks we've given them and lessen the feeling that they're being "studied."

What's great about being a UX researcher is that I get to not only see the reactions from the customer, but from the product team as well. Essentially, there's a moment being created on both sides of the glass. The customer gets to share their experience, and the product team gets a firsthand reaction to what they've built.

As you begin hacking your culture to be more customer driven, you'll realize that your work requires improvement on *both* sides of the glass. Being customer driven is about improving the overall outcome for the customer. However, to achieve this, you must invest in building a highly functional and responsive team. As I reflect on my journey of transformation with DevDiv, I realize that we've not only created an environment that honors our customers, we've also created an environment that honors one another.

Therefore, having a great employee experience is essential to having a great customer experience.

Great EX (Employee Experience) = Great CX (Customer Experience)

If your team is having a terrible experience, chances are your customers are having a terrible experience, too. If your customers are unhappy, chances are your employees aren't happy either. Creating a lasting culture that is deeply empathetic toward customer needs and experiences requires an organization that is deeply empathetic toward its employees' needs and experiences. But here's the good news: if you drive the teams toward being more empathetic with customers, there's a good chance they'll generate the skills required to be more empathetic with one another.

An interesting thing happens when I train teams in our Customer-Driven Workshop. As team members begin to talk to one another about their assumptions of the customer, they often uncover disagreements. For example, one team member thinks the feature should be targeted toward students, whereas another thinks they should be targeting faculty members. They collect some customer data and discover that neither students nor faculty members want the feature.

When each person realizes they were completely wrong, it is not only humbling, it can be a powerful moment of learning. It causes them to realize how easily their assumptions can be wrong. You can almost see them start to think, "What *other things* have I been making the wrong assumptions about?!" People have come up to me after our workshops and told me how being customer driven is a great strategy for situations outside of work. They often say that they may have been holding onto the wrong assumptions about family members, coworkers, and friends.

One gentleman, who had been in the software industry for some time, told me, "This workshop has given me a new way of looking at everything in my life. I need to slow down and not be so quick to assume everything. From now on, I'm just going to assume I don't know anything." I recall him talking about how he had been making assumptions about family members and reasons why they had drifted apart.

Although I find this sort of feedback gratifying and deeply powerful, I must be honest when I say that it has nothing to do with our workshops. Our job is to give them tools to connect with customers. That's the point of the Customer-Driven Workshop.

However, connecting with others produces a powerful moment—particularly, when you connect with people whom you thought you understood but then soon realize you have more to learn about. Running customer interviews in our workshop can produce that effect for some of our product makers.

When they get on a call and talk to a customer from another part of the world other than Redmond, our customers become real; they're not nameless, faceless users. In these moments, our workshop participants begin to realize that the customer profile they've been building in their heads was nothing like the people they met on the phone. That's a huge revelation, and it can be sincerely humbling. It might even cause you to question other areas of your life where you're making baseless assumptions.

That's what we're working toward in our workshops: to create that moment of realization for our team members, in a psychologically safe environment, so that they don't feel embarrassed but are inspired by a newfound desire to challenge every assumption they have going forward.

Agents of Change: Carmen Medina

The US Central Intelligence Agency (CIA) is responsible for collecting national security intelligence and identifying potential threats toward the United States. It's a massive endeavor generating an infinite supply of global data, which requires constant collaboration and investigation.

In the late 1990s, the CIA's ability to share knowledge and democratize data within the agency was woefully inadequate. In fact, most of the country's national security information was being disseminated on paper; many believed that using electronic systems was a sure-fire way to put sensitive materials into the enemy's hands.

Carmen Medina, a rising CIA analyst, had a proposal. Instead of printing reports on sheets of paper, intelligence agencies ought to begin publishing their findings instantaneously and transmitting them over Interlink, the intelligence community's classified intranet network.[3]

The idea was immediately dismissed by her colleagues as unrealistic. Paper was a tried-and-true method, and the internet was an unknown entity at the time. They argued that with printed reports, you could ensure that the proper officials would receive them. If you put them online, there's no telling who could access them. For the CIA, it was much more valuable to pool the information in controlled silos.

Frustrated but determined, Medina persisted. She kept bringing up the idea in meetings and advocated for the value of faster knowledge exchange. It seemed obvious that they should invest in an approach that ensured all their analysts got actionable data as quickly as possible. However, her colleagues became annoyed with her insistence. At one point, a senior-level coworker warned her, "Be careful what you're saying in these groups. If you're too honest, and say what you really think, it will ruin your career."[4]

It nearly did.

Tensions mounted, and she was forced to look for another job within the agency. She took the only job available: a staff position that was well beneath her talents and ambitions.

After the attacks on the World Trade Center in 2001, the associate director of national intelligence was confronted with a hard realization. It was becoming increasingly clear that the culture of siloed information had allowed threat warnings leading up to the terrorist attack to go unnoticed. By 2005, the calls for change were becoming magnified, and many other officers within the CIA joined Medina in her quest to open the exchange of knowledge within the organization.

Because Medina had never really put the idea down, she started speaking up again, this time with a greater organizational awareness and credibility. Together, with the help of others, Medina created a "rebel alliance." This group put forth a vision to have agents share intelli-

---

3 [Grant] p. 63
4 [Grant] p. 63

gence, much like the popular online encyclopedia, Wikipedia. The idea was that the agency could post articles and other intelligence information so that other agents could comment on it or discuss it. The associate director gave the go-ahead, and a small server was installed to try it out. Through a grassroots effort, the alliance created Intellipedia, the agency's first online knowledge network for spies.

Intellipedia is a rich and vibrant community, comprising equal parts message board, news articles, and wiki posts.

As of 2014, Intellipedia contained around 269,000 articles, 113,000 content pages, and 255,000 users.[5] It has grown into a standard part of the intelligence community's workday. It has a home page with featured and developing articles, help pages, and requests for collaboration. You can find tips on tradecraft in its pages and primers on conflicts in certain parts of the world.[6] Essentially, it's become a central hub where analysts get their daily information, search for previous reporting, and connect with one another.

Analysts agree that Intellipedia played an instrumental role in identifying terrorist threats during the 2008 Summer Olympics in Beijing. It also proved useful in tracking Russia's interference in the 2016 US presidential election.

Even though having a site with this many contributors is impressive, the website isn't the cultural element we want to focus on—it's the value of shifting to a culture that's willing to share knowledge faster and more easily.

It shouldn't take an international threat for your organization to embrace knowledge and continuous collaboration. So often, we seek to hold key information to ourselves, with a desire to maintain control or protect our teams or divisions. As the old saying goes, "knowledge is power," and if we're not careful, the knee-jerk response to withhold data twists itself into our culture like a noxious weed. Soon, you can't even explain why you're not sharing information with other workgroups; it just becomes the blanket reaction to any request for information. Although protecting customer privacy and trade secrets is incredibly important, I've found that many times, those legitimate interests can be "weaponized" and used as excuses for less collaboration.

The goal should be to protect sensitive data *and* create an environment of continuous and constant collaboration. There are many ways to anonymize customer data or provide only necessary portions of a product idea for a working group to move forward. Putting distance between the product team and its customers isn't a sustainable path forward for your business.

There are important regulations in place, and we must abide by them to earn our customers' trust. But we also must push ourselves to find appropriate and safe ways to learn and connect with our customers. For example, in our product Visual Studio, we have a feature that

---

5 [Intellipedia]

6 [Dreyfuss]

allows customers to give us feedback, directly from the product. Before collecting information about their issue, we ask the customer's permission and ask if they're willing to be contacted.

This allows us to aggregate these issues on the backend and present them to our product teams so that they can not only diagnose and fix the issues, but also get in contact with customers. These discussions can lead to even more feedback to improve the overall experience. Our customers love reporting issues this way because it keeps them in the context of their working environment. They also have a vested interest in improving the product they rely on every day, so many of them don't mind being contacted for follow-up questions, especially if they're getting help on an issue they reported. In exchange, we responsibly use their contact information and immediately remove it if the customer requests it.

I realize that this might not work under some extreme situations or regulatory constraints; however, you should still seek ways to create these types of customer and product team connections within the boundaries of what's possible for your organization. Your default mode of operation should be to move in a direction that liberates knowledge, not a direction that confines it.

Pushing for Transparency

Employees cannot effectively serve their customers when they feel like they're in the dark. Many organizations operate with little to no transparency, leaving employees with feelings of distrust between them and their organization. It's almost as if the organization doesn't believe that employees can be entrusted with sensitive business information.

That's what many people said when Jack Stack, CEO of SRC Holdings Corporation, decided to move to a radically transparent culture.

In 1983, Jack was trying to save jobs at the fledgling engine manufacturing facility located in Springfield, Missouri. The economy was in decline, the company had 89 times more debt than equity, and it was looking certain it would send more than 100 employees to the unemployment line.

Together with 12 other managers, Jack raised $100,000 and purchased the company. What he did next was inconceivable: he handed it over to the employees.

From then on, he would enforce an "open book" policy by which all employees, regardless of rank or stature, could see the company's complete financials.

He didn't stop there.

He knew that his staff would need new skills to make use of the information, so he created training programs in which employees could learn how to interpret the company's financial data. This created an environment of complete fiscal accountability. There was no way for his executive team to hide behind unearned salaries or lofty bonuses. Everyone was aware of how much money the company was making and how it chose to distribute it.

They were also aware of how much money it required to run the business. Employees started to appreciate cost-saving measures and often contributed innovative ideas to save costs and improve the business' bottom line.

"They see the relation between operations and balance sheets," Stack says. "If you teach people economic literacy, it doesn't stop with the business. It goes into their house, and into their community."[7]

Teams could see how each division created value for the company and what parts of the business needed the most help. Instead of shaming one another with financial performance metrics, employees leaned in to help one another. Stack proved that, when given the opportunity, employees would do the right thing with the information. This level of transparency and accountability heightened the willingness to share learnings because employees could see the interdependencies within the business.

Stack created an environment of trust that brought a deeper connection and meaning to employees' work. It took an incredible amount of courage on his part to trust that his employees would use the information the appropriate way.

As of 2017, SRC Holdings has grown to 1,600 employees and booked $16 million in profits on $532 million in sales the previous year. It's launched more than 60 companies in industries ranging from banking to medical devices to furniture.[8]

Admittedly, opening your financials to all your employees might be too big of an investment for your organization. Each organization has its own constraints, so there's no one-size-fits-all suggestion here. However, we must acknowledge that when employees don't have the proper information to do their jobs, it comes at a significant cost to the entire organization and, in some cases, it can dramatically affect employee morale.

Reflect on your teams' willingness to share expertise and customer learnings. Perhaps there are ways you can give one another controlled access, to achieve the security you need, without the cost of blocking essential learning from happening. In difficult situations, seek compromise and common ground. The first priority should always be customer privacy, but the second priority should be organizational learning.

The Value of a Generalist

In any system of scale, it can be important to have clearly defined functions and rules of engagement. However, you'll find that if these lines are too uncompromising, it can hinder innovation and critical thinking. Effectively, you end up in an organization so departmental-

7 [Carbonara-2]

8 [Helm]

ized and ruled by their job descriptions that you hear the dreaded phrase "that's not my job" mentioned routinely.

Unfortunately, our customers don't care at all about our organizational boundaries and hierarchy. They expect us to come together and create delightful experiences for them. If we choose to favor internal politics over our customers' needs, they will simply take their business elsewhere.

That's why we see major businesses being blindsided by scrappy newcomers all the time. These small startups aren't weighed down with the same bureaucracy and permission-seeking of their competitors. This allows their employees to wear many different hats and provide a variety of functions.

In my work in DevDiv, I've had the opportunity to talk with lots of small businesses and startups. These might be teams of 5 to 10 people, building a smartphone app, providing consulting services, or building an online service. Many of these businesses are seeking funding and are driven by a courageous vision and persistent grit. In these teams, it's not uncommon to find a shared sense of purpose and a radical diversification of duties. Backend developers will often take on frontend design work. The founder will also be the head of marketing and sales. The office manager will also handle payroll. Of course, this is mainly out of financial necessity. I'm sure if these startups had the financing to secure more head count, they would hire more specialized workers in a heartbeat.

As their companies grow, you'll begin to see the rise of the specialist. The founder might bring on someone to head the company's engineering or design efforts. They'll eventually create a position for a director of marketing. Then, they'll decide they need a team of dedicated UX researchers and designers. Little by little, the once small business becomes an organization defined by the various disciplines and divisions.

Then, innovation comes to a grinding halt. The business begins to falter by the weight of its own organizational chart. Political infighting and territorial safeguarding emerge as teams spend more time navigating interdivisional politics than on sharing knowledge or exploring the unmet needs of their customers. The role of manager becomes elevated as there's an ever-increasing demand to manage resources and standardize work. As revenues rise, managers ask for more head count to keep up with the demands of the business. Soon, teams become bloated, and tensions rise as there are only a few projects that everyone seems to want to work on. The sales division begins to grow as the business takes on top-tier clients, and account managers develop deep relationships with their customers. Meanwhile, product makers become further and further separated from the customers who use their products.

Now, I don't describe this growth pattern to demonize management or organizational hierarchy. There are more than 100,000 employees at Microsoft, and we could not function if we didn't have an organizational structure that outlined each person's responsibility. Being aware of your function within a large organization is critical to accountability. Having defined roles and clear job descriptions is necessary.

However, we must appreciate that the very systems we put in place to help us scale our business can also create distance between us and our customers. Anyone who's ever called into customer support knows the sound of the automated operator rattling off various departments as you try to decide which of them can help you with your issue.

Innovative leaders understand this, and they'll push employees to stretch the definition of their disciplines. They'll bust the "that's not my job" mentality that comes with an overreliance on specific job descriptions. They take advantage of each team member's superpower and promote diverse points of view. They'll encourage cross-functional collaboration to support a common goal rather than sabotaging an effort because it "wasn't invented on our team."

To do this, we must be comfortable with the value of being a generalist. So often, we wrap our identities around the work we do. In America, the most common question you are asked if you're meeting someone for the first time is, "So, what do you do?"

Describing one's job is a litmus test of self-worth and recognition of value. We often respond:

"I'm a developer."
"I'm a researcher."
"I'm a designer."

These roles help us define what we do, but if we're not careful, they box us in and become a limited set of who we are.

In DevDiv, we value the generalist, and we create enough flexibility for each person to stretch their expertise to meet the demands of the business.

My own personal story working in DevDiv is a prime example of this. When I was hired at Microsoft, I was listed on the org chart as a UX designer. However, throughout the years, I have been given permission to stretch the limits of what that entails well beyond what I thought was possible. I've had opportunities to train and mentor teams, design and coordinate large events, build an automated AI agent, write code and APIs, judge hackathons, host an awards show, produce and shoot short films, write books, and on and on.

Every day I'm confronted with a new opportunity and, most important, I have a leadership team that doesn't hold me back, saying, "No, you're a designer; you're only responsible for producing red lines and UI layout."

DevDiv has created an environment that utilizes each individual and allows them to contribute their talents and passions to the collective whole.

However, it took a small risk on my part. I had to buy into the idea that there was opportunity in stretching my job role—in taking on tasks that were well outside my job description. I could've leaned back and avoided projects that were not "something I was hired to do." I could've said, "I don't know how to do that, you'll need to find someone else." Thankfully, I listened to the messages from our leadership team to embrace a growth mindset. I told myself, "I don't know how to do this *yet*." Having this mindset allowed me to take risks and work on projects that were incredibly challenging but immensely rewarding. By taking a chance on projects that were not seen as "traditional software design work," Microsoft was guiding me to some of the most meaningful and impactful design work of my career.

Cross-Pollinators

In his book *The Ten Faces of Innovation*, Tom Kelley, general manager of the legendary IDEO design and consulting firm, describes the value of the *cross-pollinator*. These are individuals who have eclectic interests and are considered "T-shaped" because, although they maintain a deep knowledge and expertise in one domain, it doesn't prevent them from offering a diverse set of skills in other domains.

Kelley writes that cross-pollinators are:

> [t]he project member who translates arcane technical jargon from the research lab into vivid insights everyone can understand. They're the traveler who ranges far and wide for business and pleasure, returning to share not just what they **saw** but also what they **learned**. They're the voracious reader devouring books, magazines, and online sources to keep themselves and the team abreast of popular trends and topics. Well rounded, they usually sport multiple interests that lend them the experience necessary to take an idea from one business challenge and apply it in a fresh context. They often write down their insights in order to increase the amount they can retain and pass on to others.[9]

As I said in the opening of this book, Monty and many other mentors and leaders at Microsoft helped me appreciate the role of cross-pollinator. I began to realize that I would be much more valuable to the company if I were willing to reject boxed-in descriptions of what I was hired to do. With their guidance and support, I was empowered to achieve more.

As a leader, consider how you're taking advantage of the unique talents and passions of each of your team members:

- Are you rigidly adhering to the scope of their job descriptions or are you encouraging them to stretch and cross-pollinate their diverse experiences?
- Are you building walls around your discipline or are you creating bridges for teams to share learning and expertise?

---

9 [Kelley] pp. 69–70

- Are you rewarding team members for bringing their own "personal brand" to their discipline or are you chastising them for "being distracted"?

If you're not responsible for leading a team, reflect on how you can stretch the definition of your discipline. Consider investing in yourself by exploring additional skills that can be used by other parts of the business. The goal is to continue to "sharpen the saw," building on a set of diverse skills that make you invaluable to your organization; for example:

- If you're a designer, what was the last book you read about business?
- If you're a program or product manager, have you ever considered taking a course on design? You might understand how to request design work, but have you had the experience of staring at a blank page and trying to bring a design idea to life? These can be transformational experiences that change the way you relate and empathize with members on your team.

Having exposure to other parts of your business can improve your ability to coexperience customer learning and share that learning in immeasurable ways. You'll forge stronger relationships with your peers and establish strong bridges of mutual respect and understanding.

Finding Match Quality

In his book *Range: Why Generalists Triumph in a Specialized World,* author David Epstein writes about the notion of "match quality." This is a term that economists use to describe the degree of fit between the work someone does and who they are.[10] It's a combination of their abilities and their passions. That's the sweet spot.

As you consider roles and responsibilities in your organization (including your own), think about the flexibility that is given for employees to explore and define their own match quality. This doesn't mean you should let everyone operate completely out of scope for what they've been hired to do, but it also doesn't mean that you should strictly adhere to a prescriptive way of delivering each role in the organization.

To tackle difficult challenges, we must be willing to extend ourselves beyond what's written in our job descriptions to a degree that is appropriate for the complex problems we're trying to solve. Nebulous problems are not strictly confined to scoped, neatly-defined answers; therefore, neither should we.

---

10 [Epstein] p. 128

As employees, if we're willing to stretch ourselves beyond our roles and take on new challenges that require us to seek out new skills, we should be rewarded for those efforts.

During my time at Microsoft I have been rewarded, promoted, and given even more opportunities *because* I was willing to take the risk of finding match quality in my work.

Throughout the year, employees are asked to reflect on their performance by documenting their impact and the work they've done for the organization. The process is called Connect, and it's a useful way for me to think about the work I've done and plan, with my manager (Monty), how I intend to grow and tackle new opportunities. This continued reflection and the subsequent conversations I have had with Monty are incredibly helpful. They allow us to align, to strategize, and to ensure that I am finding match quality in my work.

The simple reality is that as we learn, we grow, and what we care about and value changes over time. I'm grateful that as I began to take on challenges that I was passionate about, I wasn't pushed out of the organization because these things weren't part of my "day-to-day duties." DevDiv saw value in what I was doing and encouraged me to continue the work even when I was feeling anxious that I had wandered too far out of scope for what the company hired me to do. As I waded into unfamiliar territory, I knew that my leadership team had my back, and that made all the difference. Being encouraged to learn and grow is a gift that any employer can give to their employees, yet so many often don't. Some leaders throw away these opportunities in favor of short-term wins or results and wonder why they are suffering from high turnover on their teams.

"Make Microsoft work for *you*" is something I've heard Satya say on numerous occasions. I just love that, because it speaks exactly to my experience in DevDiv. I was passionate about connecting our product teams to the customers they serve, and I was driven by a strong belief that, if I was willing to share my expertise with my colleagues, it wouldn't put me out of a job, but empower us all to drive empathy into the work we do.

Applying the Hack

Here are steps you can take to build bridges and tear down walls in your organization:

- When providing new methods, templates, or tools, ensure that they can be adopted easily, and check in with employees to see whether they feel successful when using them. Just like your products, test your tools with your teams. Gather feedback and adjust them to make them easier to use. Look for ways to reduce steps and increase productivity. For example, the HPF reduces complexity by streamlining the hypothesis-writing processes down to filling out a set of parameters. This significantly reduces the cognitive burden of getting started with your first hypothesis.

- Avoid "gotcha" moments in which you intentionally set teams up to learn a hard lesson. This sort of "shock therapy" rarely works, and it will cause unnecessary animosity because you've made employees feel ashamed, foolish, or stupid. Look to create moments that *build* confidence, not tear it down.

- Seed learning into the culture by giving everyone an opportunity to learn something outside their expertise. For example, our Visual Studio Code team asks *every* employee on the team to program an extension for the tool, regardless of whether they know how to write code. This not only helps new members become familiar with the product, it also gives them the chance to reach out to their colleagues for help and gain confidence in building a new skill. These aren't meaningless activities; they help employees feel connected to their customer, their product, and their workgroup.

- Treat learning as a team sport. Encourage releasing learning early and often. Real-time reporting reduces waste and overproduction. If a team can benefit from what you're working on now, show it to them—even if it's incomplete. Don't wait until you've got it perfect because many times you'll miss your window.

- Be inclusive. Look for different voices and perspectives. Make sure that teams have opportunities to coexperience learning from the customer and celebrate what they're learning.

- Actively seek partnerships with teams that are aligned with your customer-driven culture. Obsessing about the customer shouldn't be a competition. It should be something for which everyone can find an important role to play. Avoid monopolies on methods, frameworks, roles, or other ways of working. You want a global mission with flexibility to add local optimization.

- Look to diversify your specialists into generalists. When connecting with customers, encourage them to try methods that would often be seen outside their role or responsibility. Allow program managers, engineers, designers, or administrators the opportunity to formulate hypotheses, develop discussion guides, or conduct their own customer interviews to help them apply a holistic approach to product making.

- If you're leading a team, take time to learn your employees' hobbies and interests. These passions can be a great way to generate motivations. If you have a team member who's interested in painting, sculpting, making music, or baking, these are all "maker qualities" that can be channeled in a learning-first culture.

- Create opportunities for members of your team to share their passions with the team. For example, during our weekly standup, we have open time for people to share anything they might want. It's a great opportunity for team members to share ancillary interests. We've had discussions about drones, virtual reality, and graphic design. These aren't necessarily topics that affect our direct day-to-day operations, but it's a chance for a member on our team to share with us what they're passionate about. It's a great bonding experience, and we're all better educated as a result. Taking time out of our busy schedules to engage in activities like this sends a strong cultural cue to our team. Learning from one another's experiences is worth our time.

- If you're struggling to connect with another team member, consider taking them out to lunch. Changing the setting to a more personal one can often have the effect of getting them to "take their guard down" and have a more honest conversation.

- Make time available to your team to learn about other roles in your company. Giving a designer the chance to write some code or allowing a product manager to attend a sales meeting isn't a waste of time or a distraction. It's a way for them to empathize with the other roles and responsibilities of the business. It also helps them understand the impact they have on other parts of the business.

- Every time your teams are connecting with customers, it's an opportunity to invite stakeholders to witness those interactions and join in the journey of learning themselves. Consider creating opportunities where project stakeholders can hear firsthand what their teams are learning from customers.

- Ensure that the team not only collects information from customers together, but that it also analyzes the data together. For example: after a round of customer interviews, consider scheduling time for the entire team to get together in a room and review the interview notes. Each of them can mark parts of the interview that stood out to them (surprises, customer problems or frustrations, confirmations, etc.). Getting to discuss what you're learning—as you're learning it—can lead to meaningful conversations.

4

Encourage Learning Versus Knowing

As Satya Nadella accepted the role of CEO and embarked on changing the culture of Microsoft, one of the biggest challenges he encountered was getting back to the culture he had experienced more than 20 years earlier, when he had first joined the company.

In his book, *Hit Refresh*, Satya reflected on what the culture at Microsoft had become when he took the reins. "Our culture had been rigid," he remembers. "Each employee had to prove to everyone that he or she knew it all and was the smartest person in the room. Accountability—delivering on time and hitting numbers—trumped everything."[1]

My personal experience when I joined Microsoft a year before Satya took over as CEO was largely the same. I saw product teams jostle for position, trying to get their features shipped by being "airtight" and "bulletproof." There wasn't any time to talk with customers, because there were just too many specification sheets to write or meetings to discuss implementation details. Our time was consumed with trying to determine the *right way* to build something, never stopping to ask if it was the *right thing* to build in the first place. In the previous culture, the worst thing you could encounter was being proven wrong.

The individuals who succeeded in this culture were often seen as the know-it-alls. This wasn't meant to be a disparaging term, because they did, in fact, know a lot about our products, businesses, and services. That's incredibly valuable in a company with a diverse portfolio of products like Microsoft.

However, Satya was promoting a very different message. Although he valued the company's deep technical knowledge and expertise, he also needed an organization that had the capacity to renew itself and learn new things. In short, the ability to learn was more valuable than the knowledge you had already acquired.

---

1 [Nadella] p. 100

In numerous venues, I had heard Satya reference the work of Dr. Carol Dweck, one of the world's leading researchers in the fields of personality, social psychology, and developmental psychology.

In her book *Mindset: The New Psychology of Success*, she summarizes 30 years of research that confronts the idea that our qualities are carved in stone (e.g., fixed mindset). Instead, she illustrates that adaptability, innovation, and creativity stem from a fundamental belief that our abilities are elastic; that they can be improved and built upon over time (e.g., growth mindset).

Through Satya's insistence and sheer repetition, "growth mindset" became a term that shot its way through the hallways, team rooms, and board rooms.

In DevDiv, we saw this new desire to learn from customers become the "new currency" as product makers began adopting new skills and new methods to connect with customers. It became OK to admit that you didn't know something, and time was spent on strategizing new ways to learn.

Coupled with the common language of learning discussed in Chapter 2, teams were formulating experiments and conducting customer interviews, demonstrating a growth mindset and a voracious appetite to learn. Put simply: it just wasn't cool to be a know-it-all anymore. Now, it was cool to be a learn-it-all.

Our brains develop based on the output of millions of microexperiments. The learning that comes from these tiny experiments helps condition us to navigate an increasingly complex world.[2] Effectively, our minds and bodies grow by learning; why should our organization's growth be any different?

That's why promoting learning is such an important culture hack. In this chapter, we explore how cultures thrive in environments that encourage learning and psychological safety. We discuss how to make change feel safe and how to encourage others to take a risk, learn new behaviors, and join you on your customer-driven journey.

Agents of Change: Margo

It was a typical evening when Margo clocked in for her shift in the oncology ward. She had just completed a three-month-long orientation as a new registered nurse, and although she felt supported by her team, she still felt overwhelmed with all that she still had to learn.

"I had great support from my peers," she recalled, "but I was always asking questions. I was trying so hard to practice independently."[3]

She stepped into a patient's room, took his vitals, and reviewed his medication order. That's when she noticed something odd. The medication order called for 44 units of Lantus for

2 [Nap] pp. 38–39
3 [SafetyRules]

bedtime, but there was also an order for 44 units of regular insulin. She was under the impression the patient had already been given this dose of insulin, but she assumed that the process in place would've caught this order if it had already been administered.

She went to the Pyxis machine, an automated pharmacy distribution locker, placed her finger on the fingerprint scanner and collected the bags of IV medicine. "I totally relied on the computer and the system. I remember thinking, there is no way this can be in the computer and be wrong. The nurse practitioner wrote this order, a pharmacist reviewed it, and another nurse checked it.... Wouldn't the computer catch it?"

Margo reentered the patient's room and was still trying to justify why the medication order felt wrong, "I knew the order was wrong, but I was unable to say why. I told the patient, 'I have your 44 units of Lantus and 44 units of regular insulin; is that what you do at home?'"

"The patient said yes, but who knows why—maybe he was poorly educated, maybe he didn't feel empowered. I wasn't skilled enough to ask open-ended questions, so I asked for confirmation."

Margo administered the medication and went back to the floor to resume her duties.

About four hours later, she passed the patient's room and noticed his call light was on. When she walked into the room, the patient had pulled out his IV and was lying in a contorted position. He was in a full seizure and was unresponsive. She called a code blue, and a flurry of nurses and physicians rushed into the room. Everyone was asking questions, trying to determine what could've caused the seizure.

In that moment, Margo knew that to save the man's life, she'd have to own up to her mistake.

"His blood sugar is low, because I gave him too much insulin!" she finally admitted.

The staff used that information and was able to successfully resuscitate the patient. A tragedy had been narrowly averted.

The hospital administrators decided to use the situation as a learning moment for the entire hospital. They enlisted Margo to join the Root Cause Analysis (RCA) team to help unpack how the error occurred. The process required honesty and humility. She had to be willing to admit where she had made mistakes and examine why she was so reluctant to voice her concerns.

Not only did she keep her job at the hospital, she's now a well-respected nurse leader. She uses the incident to help teach other nurses about the power of speaking up and asking questions, even if it means admitting that you don't know something.

Essentially, Margo and many other nurse leaders like her are trying to chip away at the knowing culture within healthcare—the pressure to not make mistakes, to be perfect and accurate each time and in every circumstance. In Margo's case, she was aware that something was off, but she didn't have the curiosity to investigate or the courage to question the system. In social psychology, this is referred to as the bystander effect: when we are in the presence of others who are not addressing an urgent situation, we feel less inclined to intervene.

The reality is that mistakes happen all the time in healthcare. Many nurses are trained on how to avoid big mistakes, but not enough time is spent understanding how easy it is to fall into groupthink or operate on autopilot. Nursing requires a constant vigilance to question your assumptions and the willingness to speak up to ensure a patient's safety.

"In nursing school, they treat error as something really rare," Margo says. "[They show you] sensational cases, so you think that's what med error is. We need to teach nurses you *will* make mistakes."

What's remarkable about Margo's story is how the hospital dealt with the situation. Margo wasn't reprimanded or fired. In fact, she was given counseling through the hospital's Employee Assistance Network to ensure that she could process the situation in a healthy way. The organization helped her develop the courage to admit her mistake and help others learn the value of being curious and asking questions when you're unsure.

Additionally the hospital realized that Margo was an incredible asset. She had unique, firsthand, experience of how the error occurred. It could not only use her experience to correct the system, but it could also have her coach others on how to avoid the mistake she had made.

That's an exceptional example of encouraging learning over knowing.

The Importance of Acknowledging Mistakes

As part of her doctoral studies of organizational behavior at Harvard University, Amy Edmondson completed a study that followed the dynamics of teams and error reporting within two different hospitals. Her hypothesis was that teams who were more collaborative would produce fewer medical errors.

However, when she analyzed the data, she found that the opposite was true. She discovered that the teams who were more collaborative with their managers and colleagues actually produced *more* errors.[4] She wondered how that could be. It didn't make sense that teams with greater collaboration were prone to making more mistakes.

She went further into her research and uncovered the cause. It wasn't that collaborative teams were producing more errors than their noncollaborative counterparts. It was that they were *reporting* more of them.

In his book *The Best Place to Work*, Dr. Ron Friedman examines Edmondson's study and arrives at a simple conclusion. "When consequences of reporting failure are too severe," he writes, "employees avoid acknowledging mistakes altogether. But when a work environment

---

4 [Edmondson]

feels psychologically safe and mistakes are viewed as a natural part of the learning process, employees are less prone to covering them up."[5]

In collaborative environments, employees feel safe to recognize and discuss their mistakes. This leads to more error reporting. Therefore, we can't assume that when we don't see mistakes, this means they're not happening. Creating a culture that expects perfection is going to diminish employees' desire to share expertise and learning.

Edmondson says, "We need to hear from people; and yet the research, the data, are overwhelming that many people feel that they can't speak up at work."[6]

Know-it-all cultures spring from the desire to prove that you're always right or to defend a position to save face. Learning cultures require humility and the admission that you don't have all the answers.

As Edmonson uncovered, in knowledge economies and especially in product development, the landscape is constantly changing. It's virtually impossible for one person to be involved with all aspects of a product's life cycle. Therefore, you need to build teams that hold a learning-first mindset so that you ensure you're getting the most up-to-date thinking.

In this chapter, we discuss ways that you can hack your organization to a culture that values and encourages learning over knowing.

Celebrate Learning, Not Failure

When talking about building a culture that values learning, some people believe we're asking them to accept failure. They'll say, "I don't want a culture where everyone feels that failure is acceptable!"

Although failure is a pathway to learning, it can also be a signal that someone is underperforming or needs more support for the task you've assigned them. The key is determining which is which. We must decide whether what we're seeing is learning or failure. Let's explore this idea by using an imaginary scenario.

EXAMPLE SCENARIO: LEARNING VERSUS FAILURE

Let's imagine a services firm finds out that a massive potential client is considering the firm for a big project. This is an incredible opportunity for the firm, so it builds a small team to develop a compelling presentation and secure a deal with the client.

Now, let's assume that we have two teams: Team 1 and 2. Each of them is assigned this opportunity, but each team sees the opportunity differently.

---

5 [Friedman] p. 19

6 [Values]

Team 1: An opportunity to demonstrate an efficient and exacting vision

Team 1 spends the first week sorting out who is going to present to the client and in what order, saving itself valuable time to bring creative assets together. To keep decision making at a minimum, the team keeps the presentation materials locked down from the rest of the firm. It's too easy for a project like this to turn into a "design-by-committee" workshop. Keeping the working group small will streamline the decision process.

Team 1 brainstorms some ideas and is confident it has come up with a vision that will inspire not only the client, but the entire firm. After it has a rough idea in place, Team 1 consults with an outside agency to help with the creative work. The team admits that it's a bold direction, but aren't the partners always asking for more innovative ideas?

The afternoon before the client and his team arrives, Team 1 finally presents its work. In a closed-door meeting with the partners of the firm, it unveils its new media strategy as well as its presentation for the client proposal. Team 1 presents its bold strategy for the new client proposal: on the day of the client arriving, the firm will announce a pricing restructure and bundled services offering. This is something the firm's existing clients have been asking for, and announcing it the day the client arrives for the proposal will generate a lot of excitement.

The head of sales tells Team 1 that her team had already tested a similar pricing structure with some existing clients, and it received a negative reaction. She's concerned that Team 1 might have over-indexed on the value of the new bundling options in its presentation.

The head of the account management team asks whether Team 1 had a chance to connect with the client's account manager. Team 1 shuffles its response, but it's clear it hadn't. He tells the room that, from what he's heard, the client is a "numbers guy" and might have some deep questions about pricing. He suggests that the team should "stick with the pricing structure that we already know, rather than try to introduce a new model in front of an important potential client."

The pricing idea Team 1 proposes is interesting, but the firm will need more time to figure it out. Team 1 is instructed keep the new media campaign, but to stick with the current pricing structure.

Team 1 works overtime to reorganize the presentation. It removes any mentions about the new pricing ideas. To save time, the team goes with the slides that the head of sales already had. Although the story has gaps, Team 1 is resourceful, getting the last-minute information they need to propose the current pricing structure. Tensions with the other group is high, but that can always be sorted out later. After all, big proposals like this are bound to generate a bit of "politics."

The client and his team arrive. Almost immediately, the presentation is full of false starts. Just as the head of the account management team predicted, the client seems intent to ask questions around the pricing structure. Team 1 struggles to answer complex questions around pricing and services. The head of the sales team jumps in to smooth out the rough spots and they're able to continue.

With very little time remaining, Team 1 unveils the new media campaign. Rather than inspiring the client, the media appears to be boring them. One member from the client's team pulls out his phone to check his email.

When the presentation ends, the client asks for an example that demonstrates the firm's commitment to its customers. Team 1 stumbles over the answer, but the account manager was able to tell a great story that has the client smiling. The client begins to relax and engage, but time runs out. The client thanks the firm for its proposal and leaves.

There are a few follow-up attempts, but the client is never heard from again.

Team 2: An opportunity to demonstrate a learning and collaborative vision

Now, let's go through the same example scenario with Team 2.

This team starts the project by looking over the presentations the firm has given over the previous three years. One member of the team has a knack for identifying patterns in analysis. The team decides to take advantage of her strength and puts her in charge of determining whether there are any patterns that can be found in successful pitches from the past.

Through her analysis, the team discovers an interesting finding. It appears that when a sales pitch incorporates testimonials from current clients, it is accepted 78% of the time. The team is excited by this insight, but it wants to check its assumption that customer testimonials have a positive effect on the outcome of sales pitches. The team decides to share the new insight with the head of the sales team. The team lead supports the finding and suggests that she sees customers always light up when they talk about success stories from other customers.

However, she's concerned that the team's presentation is light on specifics around pricing. She's heard stories about this client. "He's a numbers guy," she says. "He's going to want to see what this all costs. It's nice to have a glitzy presentation, but make sure your numbers are rock solid." With her help, Team 2 reworks its presentation to touch on key points regarding the firm's pricing structure.

Working with the account management team, Team 2 creates a handful of customer stories that speak to the relationship the firm builds with its customers. The media is fun, authentic, and speaks to the values of the firm. When some of the sample design work is floated around the offices, people are excited and express how much they like the new messages.

The team works with marketing and design to craft a compelling theme for its presentation, calling it "The Power of Together." The presentation highlights how the firm partners with its clients to improve their businesses.

The afternoon before the presentation, the team sends out the latest version of the presentation. There's no need to meet, because many of them have been involved in helping put the presentation together. Team 2 encouraged co-discovery with their colleagues, and all that's left is to wish one another good luck.

At the beginning of the presentation, the client states that before they get to anything, he wants to discuss pricing structures. Thanks to the suggestions from the head of the sales team earlier, Team 2 was prepared and is able to confidently address the client's pricing questions and keep the presentation on track. After a series of back-and-forth questions, the client seems satisfied and begins to relax.

Seeing that he's ready to move on, Team 2 unveils its "The Power of Together" message. As part of the presentation, the team plays a video in which some of its premiere clients talk about their experiences with the firm. It's a touching video, and the partners beam as it's being played. The client smiles and nods to his team during the video. It appears to be a hit.

When the video finishes, the client says, "Wow. It's great to see what your customers think of you and see examples of what we could do together."

The client's team generally agrees, but unfortunately one member is still uneasy. He mentions that the firm has never worked with a client in the same industry as the project they're considering.

Although he was inspired by "The Power of Together" message, he wasn't sure the firm could manage this project's unique business model. The client eventually agrees that the firm might not be right for this project, but as he's leaving, he mentions to the account manager that he has another project that he believes the firm would be better suited to help with.

So in this scenario, both Team 1 and Team 2 failed to deliver the desired outcome. The client didn't choose either team's proposal for his project.

Yet, it's difficult to suggest that Team 2 failed. Even though it was unable to secure the new client, it was able to move the firm forward with valuable new knowledge. Team 2 recognized the individual talents and passions of one team member. Through her analysis, the team identified an important insight into the power of customer testimonials on sales presentations. This could be an important differentiator in how the team pitches new clients going forward.

Team 1 was not only unable to secure the client, but it left the firm in a worse position at the end of the project. The upcoming months will be consumed with infighting about changes to the pricing proposal.

With Team 1, the outcome is a lost client and a wealth of new problems. With Team 2, the outcome is a lost client, *but an exciting opportunity to improve going forward*. The team demonstrated a positive way of working, utilizing one another's strengths, and created a model of how they should engage future projects going forward.

The partners of the firm should celebrate Team 2's efforts. They should point out the innovative way in which it employed past sales presentations to gain useful insights. Congratulating Team 2 on its efforts presents an opportunity for the partners to show the rest of the firm that these sorts of calculated risks will be rewarded, even when they don't deliver the desired result. By celebrating Team 2, the partners are building the psychological safety for everyone to try new things, even in high-risk situations like pitching a big client. In this case, they can celebrate the *learning*, not the outcome. They can use this opportunity to encourage a learning mindset over a knowing one.

When successful outcomes are the only things that are recognized, employees will be more inclined to trust conservative approaches on new projects. If you want to promote innovative thinking, you must be willing to reward someone who's showing a learning mindset. Seeing examples of their peers being rewarded not only for positive outcomes but also for developing new learning for the firm, will encourage them to engage in similar risk-taking and learning-first behaviors.[7]

Lead with Questions, Not Answers

In his book *The Practice of Management*, famed management consultant Peter Drucker wrote, "The important and difficult job is never to find the right answer, it is to find the right question."[8]

To build a culture that is rooted in learning, you must be comfortable asking questions. As a leader, you might find it difficult to ask questions because you feel intense pressure to have all the answers. Many leaders believe it's their job to make the final decision and pride themselves on having enough knowledge in their given area that they are prepared to answer any question that comes their way. After all, wasn't that why they were given the leadership position in the first place?

However, the best leaders know the correct questions to ask. They not only ask questions to enrich their own understanding, but to help others learn as well. They use questions to advance debate, not to score points or make passive-aggressive arguments. For these leaders, questions are a powerful instrument that help bring clarity in complex conditions.

John Montgomery, corporate vice president, is responsible for leading all of program management, UX research, and design within the Developer Products Division at Microsoft. He believes asking questions is a powerful way to reinforce a learning mindset within his teams. John has a unique background compared to other leaders you might meet at Microsoft. He studied Russian language and literature at Harvard and even wrote articles in a variety of technology magazines for Ziff-Davis Publishing.

"My background is very different from most of the people that work at Microsoft," he says. "I don't have a computer science degree. I was never a professional software developer and so, in a lot of cases, I find myself genuinely not knowing answers to questions. My background

7 [Friedman] p. 23

8 [Drucker] p. 353

was as a journalist, and as a journalist, a lot of your job is to ask people questions to uncover what they know and to get them to tell stories."[9] Montgomery continues:

> *[The process of asking questions] very often helps [teams] see things through different perspectives and different lenses. It can move them in different directions, because they hadn't considered something. I would say [as a pattern of leadership] that question and curiosity is something I try to bring, and I try to encourage it in others.*

As a leader, John models that he's comfortable admitting what he doesn't know. He projects a curiosity and a desire to learn and he gives his reports the space to do the same.

"A completely fair answer to every question is, 'I don't know, but I can go find out,'" he admits, "and in terms of growing that, I think there is a core requirement of all program managers to approach things from that lens of asking questions."

If your organization has a strong knowing culture, it can be difficult to admit when you don't know the answer to something. In a knowing culture, people sit quietly in meetings listening to the presenter even though they have no idea what that person is talking about. Yet, when the presenter asks, "Does that make sense?" everyone nods to one another in unison.

Later, you ask a colleague, "Hey, I didn't understand the part about our new global sales quotas. Do you get that?"

Your colleague looks at you and shrugs, "Yeah, I didn't understand that, either."

You're left asking yourself, "Then why did we all agree that we understood?!" Better yet, "Why did I say *I understood*?!"

It's more than just admitting you're confused or that you need help understanding; some people feel uncomfortable asking questions because they don't want to be perceived as being difficult or wasting everyone's time. There's a fear that you might ask a question that everyone knows the answer to, leaving the group to look at you and say, "Really?! You didn't know the answer to *that?!*"

Yet, asking questions should be viewed as the ultimate sign of respect. When someone asks you a question, they're saying, "What you're saying matters to me. I want to make sure I understand you."

That's why John and other leaders who are naturally inquisitive end up creating large networks that span cross-organizational boundaries. They want the bigger picture, and they'll keep asking questions until they get it. They are shining examples of a learning culture because their pursuit of knowledge outweighs their need to create an illusion of knowledge.

---

9 [Montgomery]

In the book *The Innovator's Method*, the authors refer to these types of leaders as *chief experimenters*. These leaders rapidly test their assumptions and will often experiment by asking questions directly of the customer.

Be a Multiplier

At the start of this book, I referenced Liz Wiseman's work of identifying and unlocking the power of *multipliers*. These are people who make everyone around them smarter by helping them reveal their own ideas and discover their own potential.

Conversely, she says that *diminishers* are those who detract from others' ability to learn and grow. These individuals care more about showcasing their own knowledge and operate with an assumption that others need their expertise to solve problems. It's a vicious cycle in which they jump in on every project, offering a rapid-fire succession of opinions. Meanwhile, they lament that they're the only ones who are engaged and willing to offer ideas.

The truth is that we all are capable of being a multiplier *and* a diminisher. For example, on low-priority projects, we might be willing to allow others to step in and experiment with new ways of working, but on critical projects, we assume the role of dictator, carefully controlling the outcome. It can be challenging to maintain a growth mindset and encourage learning when projects have more importance and visibility, but it's in those moments that it's most essential to do so.

Wiseman refers to people who end up in this situation as acting like an "Accidental Diminisher." These are situations when our intention is to support others, but our actions stifle their autonomy and creativity.

It's true. When I'm excited about an idea, I leap first and stitch the parachute on the way down. I fully admit that it can be an exhausting personality trait to be around. In many ways, this behavior can have diminishing effects. If you're an idea-generating machine like me, be aware that you might be exhausting your colleagues. If you're in meetings and you're the only one proposing ideas, perhaps you're diminishing others' ability to process the conversation and jump into the discussion. Try taking breaks or asking others about their ideas.

One experiment that Wiseman suggests is to "play fewer chips." Essentially, if you know you're going to go into a meeting that will require a lot of ideation, try giving yourself a mental count of how many chips you're willing to use. Each chip represents a comment, suggestion, or idea. If you go into a meeting with a plan to spend only five chips, you might find that you are far more judicious with your feedback.

What I've come to realize is that the energy I have around ideation is infinitely more valuable and rewarding when I use it to help *others* generate their own ideas. Multipliers build on the superpower of those around them. They improve collaboration and overall performance of the team by doing the following:

- Asking questions to encourage learning, not to encourage skepticism
- Operating with an assumption of positive intent and a belief that ideas are better when influenced by multiple perspectives
- Championing the work of others as they build on top of their efforts
- Resisting the urge to discount the ideas of others because they value multiple points of view

According to Wiseman's research of more than 150 executives across the Americas, Europe, Asia, and Africa, the "Multiplier Effect" had the power to double, and in some cases nearly triple, the productivity and output of teams.

Employees of multipliers were more engaged, more innovative, took more risks, and were more satisfied with the work they were doing. The research confirmed that multipliers not only access people's current capability, they stretch it. They get more from people than they knew they had to give. Employees reported actually getting smarter around multipliers.[10]

Consider situations in which you can encourage others by being a multiplier. Are there situations when you're acting like a diminisher? It might be worth asking coworkers you trust to give you an honest assessment. Perhaps you're unintentionally behaving in a way that is diminishing others.

Is your cultural change effort languishing because it's more important for your team to showcase its knowledge rather than to build a platform for the ideas of others?

Monty told me once that "the quickest way to gain influence over others is by helping them get promoted." It's a bit of a joke with a strong thread of truth woven into it. Bottom line, people are more receptive to your ideas if you're building on the work they're doing. They'll be more willing to share what they're learning and contribute if they believe you're investing in their growth.

When working with others, consider spending time reflecting on their superpower. Perhaps it's something they do that they don't even realize is valuable. If they don't see their own value, be sure to point it out to them. These are opportunities to invest in others and help them build on their strengths. You'll not only get more out of them, but you'll find they are far more willing to invest in your change effort.

To encourage a change movement, you need to get into the business of multiplying others' strengths rather than constantly pointing out their weaknesses.

---

10 [Wiseman] p. 12

Creating the Space to Learn

If you want others to own the job of learning, you must give them a safe space to experiment and learn from their findings. Mistakes and miscalculations will happen—it's inevitable in any business. Exploring one's mistakes is a necessary part of learning, and it starts from being able to admit you were wrong and it ends with being given the opportunity to adjust your approach.

That's what's so great about using a language of learning and adopting the hypothesis as the instrument to engage in coexperienced learning. When your culture trades in hypotheses instead of ideas, you find that employees are able to separate their identities from their ideas, which makes them easier to discard when they've been proven wrong.

"Ideas are things you can fall in love with," says John Montgomery.

Hypotheses are disposable, in fact, a great hypothesis is designed to be proven wrong. The more hypotheses we have that we can invalidate, the better off we are, because that's work that we don't have to do. In an environment where resources are finite, knowing that you don't have to do some collection of work, is tremendously powerful.[11]

It's painful to see teams lose a valuable contributor because they had the audacity to try something novel and it didn't produce the desired result. Many times, these people feel that the only way to save face after a mistake is to leave the company or team.

So how do you prevent that from happening?

- If you're a leader, the first and most profound way to encourage psychological safety is by demonstrating it. Be willing to admit where you were wrong or where you had to correct your thinking. Give credit to those who've helped you learn, even if it's someone who reports to you. If it's someone in a junior position or someone who just joined your team, even better. Showing this level of humility will not only make you a great leader, it will show your team that you value learning. Modeling that you're willing to learn when proven wrong is the best way to encourage the same behavior within your team.

- If you're not in a leadership position, be sure to support your colleagues and celebrate how they've helped you learn. A fantastic way to build a culture of trust and connection is by pointing out what you're learning from the people you're working with. It not only makes them feel helpful, but it also demonstrates that you're willing and capable of learning new things. If a project fizzles out, instead of covering up what went wrong, spend time reflecting on what you learned and share those lessons with your coworkers.

---

11 [Montgomery]

Engage with others by asking for feedback. An undesirable outcome is the best opportunity to make a discovery and learn something new.

Too many times, status meetings drone on as people go through their inventory of accomplishments and project work. It's a way to signal to everyone how busy and successful they are. Pretty soon, you're saying to yourself, "Susan sounds like she's really busy and important. Look at all the projects she's working on! I'd better update my list so I sound busy, too!"

There are better alternatives to these types of meetings.

At the dinner table, our family plays the game "Rose, Bud, Thorn." Essentially, you go around the table and have each person describe three things:

- Rose: Something that went great today.

- Bud: Something that you're excited about.

- Thorn: Something that's causing you frustration, anxiety, or pain.

It's a great way for us to unpack one another's days, celebrate the things that are going well, revel in the excitement of things to come, and support one another through things that are causing worry or pain.

Consider trying this game or some variant of it during your next status meeting. Instead of everyone giving a complete list of everything they're working on, scope it to three items: something successful, something promising, and something frustrating. It's a great way to just get to the point and focus the team's energy on celebrating success and providing support.

It's also a way to create a psychologically safe environment for team members to talk honestly about where they need help or suggestions. It's an opportunity to say, "You know what? I'm frustrated by something and I could use some help."

It might feel awkward or forced at first; that's OK. As people begin to become more comfortable sharing their status in this way, you'll find that resistance will begin to soften.

Collaboration isn't always sunshine and rainbows. As we discussed in Chapter 1, there are times when you'll need to "fight and unite." It's important to remove threatening language when collaborating. Avoid using extreme language (e.g., "You never...," "You always...") and ask questions that foster more understanding (e.g., "Tell me more about..."). However, it must be stated that this technique can be manipulated. If you're asking questions just to poke holes into someone else's idea, that can be easily spotted. If I have a question after someone has presented a new idea, I like to say things like, "I'm not asking this to challenge your idea, I want to better understand what you're proposing." A simple comment like this can diffuse questioning and help the presenter understand that I'm here to help make their idea better. Presenting new ideas takes courage, and diffusing my language when asking questions helps the conversation stay collaborative. If I demonstrate humility during collaboration, I'm much more likely to see that behavior reciprocated by the person with whom I'm trying to collaborate.

Break the Script

Sometimes, you'll find yourself in a situation in which the team is burnt out or morale is low. Perhaps they're struggling after a disappointing launch or they're lacking the inspiration to generate new ideas. They're just stuck in a rut. In these moments, consider trying something radically different in terms of triggering another wave of learning. It can be something that "shocks the system" or simply breaks the monotonous day-to-day routines.

In 2011, Microsoft Corporate Vice President of Cloud and AI, Scott Guthrie, did just that. At that time, he was leading the group responsible for Microsoft Azure, the company's ambitious cloud-computing platform. The competition was stiff as Amazon had garnered significant market share with its Amazon Web Services (AWS) platform. Both companies were throwing their weight behind their respective platforms because the cloud business space represented the future of applications and services.

Although Azure presented a unique value proposition that helped customers move to the cloud more gradually by taking advantage of their previous Microsoft investments, its users were frequently complaining that Azure was difficult to use.

Guthrie decided to hold an offsite meeting and asked all of his senior leaders to attend. When they arrived, he had a simple request.

"Basically, the deal was all the senior managers and architects had to bring their laptops, and we were going to build an app from scratch together for two days," Guthrie says. The goal was simple: he wanted his key executives to go through exactly what Azure customers go through when trying to get started with the service.

"It was a complete disaster," Guthrie said.[12] For two days, the organization's highest-ranking people struggled with basic tasks like getting their account set up and deploying their first app. It was a shocking revelation.

In their book *The Power of Moments: Why Certain Experiences Have Extraordinary Impact*, authors Dan and Chip Heath refer to this moment as "tripping over the truth."

Essentially, Guthrie needed to break the script. He had to create a moment when his leadership team and creative leaders were faced with the cold, hard truth: their customers were struggling with Azure. These issues were no longer up for debate; if the top people at the company couldn't use the product successfully, how could they expect their customers to be successful?

---

12 [Nusca]

For the team, the shame they felt in that moment had a lasting impression. By the second day, they had compiled more than 100 items that needed to be fixed. They came up with a plan to correct the issues and spent the following year building upon what they had learned.

Guthrie had helped his team empathize with its customers' frustrations because he took team members out of their day-to-day environments and had them experience what it was like to struggle with getting started with Azure. Because they had felt the pain for themselves, their mission was lasting and tangible. As soon as they felt the customer's pain, they couldn't forget it. They were now compelled to fix the issues.

"We spent the next year completely rebuilding Azure," Guthrie remembers. "It was fun because people could see the progress. People could feel the energy."

Consider how you might build similar moments for your team to have a learning that surprises them. Many times, our teams are so convinced that they have all the answers, their egos can benefit from a small dose of humility.

Having them complete common scenarios using the product you're building or spend time with a customer who's never used the product before can be great ways to quickly build empathy. Look for those moments to inspire others into action.

Yes, and...

Collaboration and ideation are critical tools that should be encouraged in your culture of learning.

A classic game that's played in improv groups all around the world is *Yes, and*. Essentially, the object of the game is to continually add to the scene being built from the various players.

For example, one player—let's call her Alisha—might sit on the ground and pretend to cast a fishing line out on an imaginary lake. She says, "Hey James! You think we're going to catch the big one today?"

The next player—James, in this case—must creatively *add* to the scene he's been given. He needs to work with her idea of fishing at the lake and add an element to keep the story going. James sits down next to Alisha, pretends to open his tackle box, and says, "Yes, and I think we're gonna have a good shot 'cuz I brought this here special bait I made!"

When performed in front of an audience, the crowd delights in how each player quickly adds to the scene, building the story together, right there on stage.

What's powerful about this technique of ideation is that it forces each person to build on the idea of the other. In meetings, it's too easy to jump in and squash a creative session by critiquing an idea before it has time to flourish. The proverbial "that will never work" gets uttered and the brainstorming session comes to a grinding halt.

In a culture that encourages learning, you need to build the patience that's required to let others explore their ideas.

Many times, we're quick to want to add value to a discussion, but often, the best way to provide value is to listen and only ask questions to help others clarify their ideas.

During your next collaboration meeting, play a little game with yourself. Try only *adding* to everyone else's idea and not submitting one of your own. Notice how it will require you to listen intently and be fully present in the room. You'll get out of your own head because you won't be constantly comparing your ideas to those of your peers. Your entire focus will be on enriching the ideas of others, shedding what you know, and preparing yourself to learn something new.

Applying the Hack

Here are some ideas you can use to encourage learning over knowing in your teams and throughout your organization:

- Genuinely celebrate invalidated hypotheses. When a hypothesis has been invalidated, it's a discovery—not a situation for which a team has failed to predict the outcome.

- Create a library. Create an atmosphere in which team members are sharing books and online articles.

- Consider using physical books in your library. You can tag pages or highlight important findings. The books become a physical manifestation of where the team has collected its learning. It's also a powerful belonging cue to anyone joining your team. A bookcase full of highlighted books and reports screams, "We love learning new things here!" These books are tangible and visible. They're not tucked away in some folder on your PC, but available to anyone who happens to be walking by.

- Openly question overstated confidence and encourage continued experimentation.

- Publicly thank those who offer a different opinion than yours. Even if you don't agree, you should acknowledge the courage it takes to present an alternative point of view.

- Don't make points through questioning. It's passive aggressive and easily spotted. Use questioning as a genuine way to seek understanding and clarification. If you have a point to make, just make it openly and respectfully.

- During status meetings, consider playing a game like "Rose, Bud, Thorn." Each team member goes through their status by picking one thing that is going well (Rose), one thing that's promising (Bud), and one thing that's causing them frustration or anxiety (Thorn).

- In your next collaborative discussion with your team, consider *only* building off the ideas of others and resist adding a new idea of your own. You can play a game of "Yes, and," essentially limiting yourself and others to responses that start with "yes." Brainstorming in this way forces your brain to look for a way to add to someone else's idea rather than state a problem with it.

- Check your ego. When you've made a misstep or mistake, own it. In moments of failure, we have an opportunity to show our best selves and demonstrate the culture we want to have. Don't shy away from mistakes—embrace them as an opportunity to model learning from one's mistakes.

Build Leaders That Build Your Culture

Rather than have a culture that celebrates *"failing* fast,"* you should consider building a culture that celebrates *"learning* fast."* Celebrating experiments that can be directly tied to revenue results is easy; it's tangible. However, trying to uncover learning that isn't directly tied to a revenue number is much more difficult. These learnings are just as valuable because they invalidate our hypotheses and help us avoid costly mistakes.

Yet, so many product teams still celebrate only when a product or feature ships on time.

I've talked with many product team members who become frustrated because they've felt like they did all the requisite customer research, but it didn't result in a business opportunity. They feel their work is wasted because it didn't produce a product to sell or a feature to ship. What they don't often appreciate (and I often remind them) is that they helped move the organization forward. While their experiments might not have produced a product worthy of putting into the market, it did give us other valuable insights. Learning what's *not* worth building is just as valuable as learning what is.

Throughout this book, I've made the case that being customer driven is actually being *learning* driven. Therefore, a customer-driven culture is one that builds leaders who are willing to learn.

In this chapter, we explore why developing leaders who demonstrate the vital behaviors of your culture is a useful hack in building a customer-driven culture.

Model, Coach, Care

We've been discussing the three vital behaviors of change (awareness, curiosity, and courage) as the foundational behaviors that are directly tied to change. However, if you want those behaviors to go viral within your organization, you must engage in three additional behaviors: *model*, *coach*, and *care*.

In fact, at Microsoft, management training is based on a model, coach, and care framework. This framework defines the three behaviors as follows:

Model

>Set the tone for culture and leadership

>Act with integrity

>Be accountable

Coach

>Define team objectives and outcomes

>Enable success across boundaries

>Help the team adapt and learn

Care

>Know everyone's capabilities and aspirations

>Attract and retain great people

>Invest in the growth of others

Essentially, managers at Microsoft are expected to invest in learning and the development of others. One of the most powerful ways they can encourage their team to adopt a growth mindset is by modeling the mindset themselves, coaching it in others, and caring about the individuals on their team.

Agents of Change: Julia Liuson

Corporate Vice President of Developer Division Julia Liuson is a perfect example of a leader who models, coaches, and cares about the customer-driven, learning-first mindset at DevDiv.

For example, I've had the benefit of seeing her in numerous settings in which she'll admit when her idea is only an assumption that hasn't been tested. When she models this behavior, it's a powerful moment because she's indirectly telling us, "I'm still learning," and it makes it OK for us to admit that we're still learning, too. When you work with Julia, learning becomes the objective—knowing does not.

In product review discussions, she coaches teams by asking questions that spark their curiosity. It's not uncommon to hear her ask questions like, "Which customers have you talked to?" and, "How do we know this feature solves the problem for the customer?" or, "What are your hypotheses?" She's not only asking these questions to determine how connected the team is to its customers; she's also modeling to the team what she values most: learning from our customers.

Getting to know Julia, I've realized that learning is an essential part of how she works. For her, learning is a strategic advantage and part of how she sees the world.

Julia Liuson was born in Shanghai, China, but grew up in Beijing during the mid-1970s. It was a poignant time of change for that country as it began its journey toward digital transformation, moving toward a modern economy.

Julia's mother and father were academics, working as faculty members within the halls of the prestigious Beijing University. Her father was a mathematician and her mother specialized in software and hardware engineering.

During this time, the Chinese government was looking for top talent within its university system to help modernize the country and compete with the explosion of technology innovation in the United States. Julia's mother was selected to work on an incubation project that explored how to bring complex Chinese characters to modern printing processes, like laser and thermal printing. The head of the project was Professor Wang Xuan, who was a legend within the Chinese tech community. Julia remembers him frequently stopping by her family's apartment to discuss new ideas with her mom. Together, Julia's mom and Professor Xuan's work eventually established an industry standard in Chinese printing that contributed to the success of many well-known Chinese tech companies, like Toshiba and Lenovo.

These were formative years for Julia, and she was surrounded by learning.

In 1987, when she was ready to leave for college, the cultural revolution was coming to an end in China, and it was very difficult to leave the country. Food was being rationed and only residents of major cities had the right to buy their own goods and services.

Julia still had a strong desire to develop her education, so in light of these challenges, she boarded her first-ever plane ride and traveled to the United States to study at the University of Washington.

When she came to America, it was a bit of a culture shock.

"My host parents took me to see Pike Place Market," Julia recalls, "I was, like, 'OK, so it's a market.'"[1]

To her, Seattle's iconic farmer's market, which is renowned for its employees who toss fish through the air to enthusiastic tourists, was like any other market in China, and she'd seen plenty of those.

"Then I went see Safeway afterward," she continues, "and I was completely shocked. There was nothing like that anywhere. It was so big, with shelves and shelves of merchandise. You could just push a cart and grab whatever you want. That, to me, was a culture shock."

Julia uses her own personal stories to help product teams appreciate the value of diverse experiences. She says that these stories help them appreciate that they often overvalue their own experiences, and if left unchecked, they can bring their own biases into their product making.

---

1 [Liuson]

At the University of Washington, she had access to technology and eventually pursued a degree in electrical engineering. She was introduced to programming and began using Applesoft BASIC (a dialect of Microsoft BASIC) and Microsoft DOS, Microsoft's earliest operating system.

She'd later join Microsoft as an entry-level engineer, working on Project Cirrus, the company's first attempt to sell a relational database product. The project would later become known as Microsoft Access.

At the time, she wasn't even sure she was going to stay at Microsoft. "I was debating about going to grad school. I was waiting for grad school acceptance. I said, 'Well, let's see how this thing goes, if I like it, I'll stay, if not I'll go.'"

Clearly, it turned out to be an opportunity that she liked. Twenty years later, she would become the corporate vice president of DevDiv. When asked why she stayed, her answer is simple.

"It became clear that within the first couple of months, I was going to get paid to learn," she says. "That's what impressed me. Within the first couple of months, I had learned so much from just doing day-to-day work and that was, like, wow! That was amazing."

As a leader, she has taken that value of learning, one of Microsoft's greatest benefits to its employees, and made it a centerpiece for her organization. Many times, she instructs teams to go out into the world and learn from what others are doing—to reject our hubris and learn from others' success.

[When thinking of solutions], we need to move away from a mentality where we have to invent everything ourselves. What other implementations are out there? How do other companies do this?

During engineering reviews, she makes it a practice to constantly ask, "What have we learned?" She believes that it takes the emphasis off employees trying to prove what they already know or finger-pointing at each other to avoid responsibility.

My questions are highly predictable. I'm going to ask, what have you learned? What customers have you talked to? What are they trying to do? What are their challenges? Has anyone else solved this problem?

After a while, teams begin to get the picture. They can't keep coming into reviews without answers to these questions. Julia is leading through the questions she asks. Those questions are an indication of what she values and what she wants the culture to value, as well. With a combination of the questioning and modeling, Julia is sending strong belonging cues to her employees. She's signaling through language and her own behaviors what it means to be part of DevDiv.

Beyond modeling a learning mindset, Julia also looks for opportunities to celebrate teams that are investing in the customer-driven culture of learning.

"Julia does an amazing job of showing up as curious, as empathetic, and as empowering," says Amanda Silver, Partner Director of Program Management in DevDiv. "She does a really great job of managing through positive reinforcement. When she sees the behavior that she's seeking, she celebrates it and shares it broadly. Even in cases where she's not thrilled with the result, she'll frame it as a learning opportunity."[2]

As an influencer of change, it's your job to seek out, mentor, and give visibility to the individuals who exemplify the new culture you're trying to build. People in your organization need examples of the behaviors they need to copy in order to belong to the new culture. Therefore, you should look for ways to build leaders who are bound to vital behaviors of your new customer-driven culture.

Celebrating the Vital Behaviors

Earlier in the book, we discussed the three vital behaviors for culture change: awareness, curiosity, and courage. Although these are the essential behavior patterns that bring about change, you should be on the hunt for anyone who is exemplifying observable behaviors that fall into those three categories.

For example, it might be highlighting a team that demonstrated the curiosity to develop a new process, allowing them to better connect with customers. Or sharing the story of a team's courage to admit that they launched a feature that customers initially resisted, but after listening to their feedback and making changes, customers began to adopt.

By shining a spotlight on these stories, you give your organization vivid examples of what the new culture looks like.

It's much more than creating an "Employee of the Month" program that requires managers to nominate outstanding employees. It's about highlighting the success of others through story. Companies that are built on top of a foundation of connecting with customers provide avenues for employees to share their own stories of success and customer learning.

Bruce Broussard, CEO of Humana, an American health insurance company based in Louisville, Kentucky, uses stories of exceptional customer service to inspire employees and highlight the vital behaviors he wants to see throughout his organization.

Humana has more than 41,000 employees and in 2018 was ranked 56 on the Fortune 500 list. What started as a nursing home in 1961 has become a massive managed care network, primarily focused on assisting elderly Medicare patients. Humana's goal is to help employers

---

2 [Silver-2]

navigate healthcare costs as well as reduce costs for patients by rewarding them for engaging in behaviors that lead to healthier lives.

To show employees what this looks like in practice, Broussard regularly shares the story of a Pharmacy Solutions employee who was working with a patient diagnosed with a diabetic condition. The patient explained that he was not only struggling to pay his pharmacy bills but was also struggling to buy food that wouldn't aggravate his condition. Maintaining a healthy eating plan to keep his diabetes in check was proving to be prohibitively expensive.

Humana doesn't want to just be a provider of healthcare; rather, it wants to be a partner with its members in seeking solutions that affect their care. Situations like this are all too common for their elderly members; they find their health in jeopardy due to negative social determinants like food insecurity, loneliness, and isolation. With its "Bold Goal" program, Humana seeks to apply a holistic approach to healthcare.

Under this program, the employee decided to take it upon herself to connect the patient to another group at Humana. That very same day, the employee and her coworkers contacted a local food bank to deliver healthy groceries to the patient, free of charge. For the patient, what started as a call to figure out his pharmacy bills resulted in an act of generosity and empathy from the Humana team. It was a powerful moment for both the patient and the company.

William Fleming, President of Healthcare Services at Humana, reflects on how this employee's actions were a direct reflection of the company's culture:

> *The point here is that, had we not established a culture in which this employee felt the freedom to extend herself beyond her routine duties, this member may not have been helped in all the ways needed. She felt comfortable not only thinking outside of the box but finding and connecting to resources in a different part of the organization, while keeping the end goal—helping our member—her North Star.[3]*

With its Bold Goal initiative, Humana created a culture that encouraged employees to be aware, curious, and courageous. This employee applied all three to deliver an indelible experience for one of its members.

The company wanted to highlight this story for all employees to reflect on and aspire to. It became a sort of legend; the story made the rounds in leadership meetings, the intranet, and was featured on a company podcast.

By celebrating the vital behavior or thinking of the Humana member as a human in need rather than a person to charge and collect money from, it gave all employees a roadmap to mirror desired behavior. It gave them a framework of what it looks like to belong to the Bold Goal

---

3 [Fleming]

philosophy of the company. The courageous actions of a single employee created a script for the rest of the company's 41,000 employees.

In our Customer-Driven Workshops in DevDiv, we spend three to four days with new employees as they work together in groups on a real business goal that has been given to them by our leadership team. As we discussed in Chapter 1, the business goals they are given are audacious and broad. The goal is to get them engaged in deep conversations and learning from the customers and one another. Essentially, it's a few days to be immersed in the framework and tools we've written about in *The Customer-Driven Playbook*.

Here's a bit more about how the week develops:

Day 1

> Teams evaluate and discuss their business goal. They identify their assumptions about the customer, their motivations, the behaviors customers engage in to achieve their goals, and the problems they encounter. Then, they formulate those assumptions into hypotheses and create a set of questions to interview customers to validate or invalidate their assumptions.

Day 2

> Teams get a chance to talk to three to four real customers who have already been scheduled in advance. After the customer interviews, teams engage in sense-making exercises and discuss what they've learned.

Day 3

> Teams talk more deeply about the unmet needs they uncovered during their customer interviews (or any other relevant data they've discovered). They begin to ideate on potential solutions and prioritize how those solutions can affect the customer and our business.

Day 4

> The final day is what we affectionately refer to as the "Science Fair." Members from our leadership team attend and teams get a chance to present their learnings by using their "Journey Wall," a low-fidelity collection of learnings affixed to a portion of the wall in the room.

There are a handful of moments during the week that always deliver meaningful results for our participants. Being able to work on a real business goal, working together in teams and making things, and getting a chance to connect with real customers are always highlights.

However, it cannot be overstated how important the final day is. When our leaders show up and invest their time to hear from what these new employees learned from our customers, it sends a *massive* belonging cue. It tells every new employee, "We care about what you've learned from our customers."

After seeing each team's presentation, the members of our leadership team pick a team as the "winner." They frame the decision based on the team they believed best exemplified the three vital behaviors (awareness, curiosity, and courage). Teams that demonstrate an awareness of their own assumptions, show gumption or a willingness to experiment or find new sources of information, or teams that have the courage to challenge the leadership team on the business goal itself are all worthy candidates for being selected as winners.

In some cases, our leadership team will pick three winners, one for each vital behavior. The winners typically attend a lunch with John Montgomery, corporate vice president and head of program management in DevDiv. Although a lunch is a relatively small gesture, having the chance to meet, face-to-face, with a senior leader, especially because you exhibited desirable cultural behavior, is a powerful moment that encourages our teams to continue to invest in our vital behaviors.

Scripting the Vital Behaviors

Although stories are an excellent vehicle to inspire the vital behaviors of awareness, curiosity, and courage, it won't be enough to help employees internalize it. Change can be paralyzing. You can't very well go out and ask your employees to be courageous or more curious. They need a smaller set of instructions that helps them align to the greater organizational mission.

Sociologists refer to public-facing goals, such as Satya's mission statement to empower every person and organization on the planet to achieve more, a *manifest function*. This is the reason that Microsoft exists. However, all the other goals that derive from that mission—goals that might not be expressed explicitly—are *latent functions*. The goal of any organization or team is to take the manifest function of the organization and derive a set of latent functions that employees can utilize in their day-to-day work.

An example of this can be found on Interstate 10, between San Antonio and Houston.

If you're driving along that route, you'd be hard pressed to miss a series of billboards for Buc-ee's (Figure 5-1), a massively popular, Texas-owned chain of convenience stores. One sign might read: "Jerky. One of the five basic food groups," or, "Only 262 miles to Buc-ee's. You can hold it," or, "Everything is fresh, even the junk food."

As the saying goes, "Everything is bigger in Texas," and it would certainly hold true for Buc-ee's. In 2012, Buc-ee's unveiled the world's largest convenience store by building a 67,000-square-foot megaplex in New Braunfels, Texas. That's 20 times larger than your average convenience store and longer than an American football field. The store touted 60 gasoline pumps, 84 toilets, 80 soda dispensers, 31 cash registers, 23 flavors of its signature fudge, and an endless maze of popcorn, candy, beef jerky, and other roadside snacks.[4] In Katy, Texas, the company is listed in the *Guinness Book of World Records* as having "the world's largest drive-through car wash."

Figure 5-1. Buc-ee's gas station in Temple, Texas (credit: Stacy Huggins)

The roadside stops are famous in the region and have a cult-like following. This has caused the chain to expand well beyond the founder's initial plans. As of this writing, Buc-ee's has 37 locations after eventually branching outside of Texas into Alabama and Florida. Customers love Buc-ee's-branded merchandise, teenagers wear T-shirts emblazoned with the store's iconic beaver, and it's not uncommon for tourists to show up and take selfies in front of the store. However, one signature attraction stands out above all the rest: Buc-ee's claims to have the nation's cleanest bathrooms.

In a travel study conducted by GasBuddy, 37% of drivers said one of their worst fears of traveling on the road was being "unsure of where to stop for a clean restroom."[5]

---

4 [Bustillo]

5 [ABC13]

That's why Buc-ee's travel centers have restrooms with large entryways that are decorated with Texas-themed memorabilia. They have high ceilings and bright lighting. The toilets are separated not by thin dividers, but actual walls that support heavy metal doors.[6]

Buc-ee's co-owner, Arch "Beaver" Aplin III, keeps the mission and goal simple: "Be clean, be friendly, and be in stock."

Even though the chain of gas stations might be a complex operation, the core mission for all employees is simple. They must be constantly friendly, keep the shelves full, and obsess over cleanliness.

That's why restrooms are staffed 24 hours a day, 365 days a year, by uniformed employees whose sole focus is to keep them immaculate. The mission isn't to sell Buc-ee's-branded food or merchandise, nor is it to have the lowest prices on gas (although Buc-ee's does strive for those things). It's to have a safe, clean refuge for customers traveling on the road.

Aplin could've easily been distracted by the myriad ways to serve customers, coming up with gimmicks like discounted prices or branching out to as many locations as his balance sheet would allow, but he decided to obsess over the things that travelers cared most about, like clean restrooms.

"Be clean, be friendly, and be in stock," might indeed be the *manifest* function for Buc-ee's, but the *latent* function is to have the cleanest bathrooms of any gas station in America. Latent functions take the broader mission and break it down to its more actionable goals. It provides a roadmap for employees to engage in smaller actions but provide support to the larger mission. It makes achieving the mission far less daunting because it prescribes what behaviors to obsess about. In the case of Buc-ee's, one of the ways that you can participate in Aplin's mission to be clean, friendly, and in stock is to obsess over the cleanliness of the bathrooms.

Do Less, Then Obsess

In a study conducted of 5,000 managers and employees across a wide range of jobs and industries, it was discovered that participants who engaged in a "do less, then obsess" mentality performed 25 percentage points higher in performance ranking compared to those who did not engage in this activity.[7] Essentially, those who picked a strategy and obsessed over it did better than those who pursued multiple strategies and goals.

In the book *Switch: How to Change Things When Change is Hard*, authors Dan and Chip Heath refer to this concentration of core ideas as "scripting the critical moves."[8] The key is to find the right moves for your organization. "Be clean, be friendly, and be in stock" is perfectly

---

6 [Carbonara]

7 [Hansen] pp. 19

8 [Heath] pp. 49–72

crisp and clear for a franchise of convenience store employees, but far too constraining at a company like Microsoft.

In *The Customer-Driven Playbook*, we highlighted the key behaviors to be consistently applied at all stages of the HPF. As the book became more widely used in DevDiv, it gave teams a script of behaviors to drive customers into their day-to-day work. The script was simple: we formulate our assumptions into hypotheses, we run experiments to validate or invalidate those hypotheses, and we apply sense-making techniques to identify patterns and insights.

As discussed in Chapter 2, the *customer-driven cadence* is applied through each stage of the HPF. Essentially, the cadence scripts learning behaviors throughout the entire development life cycle of our products, as demonstrated in Figure 5-2.[9]

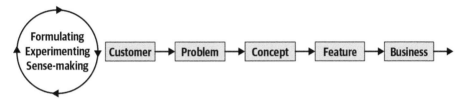

Figure 5-2. The customer-driven cadence is applied to all stages of the HPF

This cadence acts as one of the many ways we script the vital behaviors in our organization. The cadence functions as a consistent model of behaviors that can be applied to any problem. You can also relate this customer-driven cadence to the language of learning we discussed in Chapter 2 (see Figure 2-1).

During product engineering reviews, teams give our leaders updates on the progress of their projects by sharing the status of their hypotheses. This practice has proven to be an effective way to communicate where the team's current thinking is and what they have learned.

Consider how you might distill your organization's mission statement into a set of key behaviors that everyone can identify and adhere to. These distillations can be highly effective in helping groups put the organization's mission into action.

Demonstrate Your Values Through Belonging Cues

To understand the impact of belonging cues, let's explore an imaginary scenario in which a new employee navigates her first day on the job.

---

9 [Lowdermilk-Rich] pp. 9–10

EXAMPLE SCENARIO: ADRIANA'S FIRST DAY

In this scenario, Adriana, our new employee, has accepted a job as a junior sales associate on a large sales team for an even larger organization. On her first day at the company, she enters the building, excited and nervous. This job represents the opportunity she's been waiting for, and she can't wait to meet her new team. She's a bit frazzled, however, because she just spent the last 20 minutes trying to figure out where to park. Even though it's a bit embarrassing, she reassures herself that these sorts of things are expected on someone's first day.

As she walks up the stairs to where she thinks her new team is, she's already noticing that she's overdressed. She's wearing a suit, while everyone around her is dressed down in business casual.

"It's OK," she says, trying to convince herself. "I'll just look like I'm eager to make a good impression."

After a few wrong turns, she finally enters the team room and immediately begins to scan the large space, looking for a familiar face. It's a maze of cubicles and it's impossible to see anyone beyond the tiny barriers.

It's been two months since she interviewed for the job, so the only face she remembers is her hiring manager's. From what she can see, she's not in yet, so she walks through each cubicle, looking for a space that might be her future home. She finds an empty, unmarked cubicle and because she's starting to feel a bit embarrassed, she decides to sit down and wait for her manager to arrive.

It's still early, but the office is already buzzing with activity. She can hear the trill of phones ringing softly throughout the office.

As people walk by, they avoid eye contact. They appear to be too busy to engage in pleasantries. Adriana decides to read through a pamphlet that was sent to her home after she had accepted the position. The document is mostly boilerplate, predictable, and uninspired. It's full of platitudes and obvious statements around the company's dedication to employees and its customers. It also champions what appears to be a new "culture movement" at the company. It walks through the "three pillars of success": family, pride, and customer service.

It extols the virtues of "maintaining a work–life balance that is healthy for you and your family." It outlines how the company is "one big family" and that "it's important to embrace diversity and respect others." Adriana's parents were Cuban immigrants, and she finds it ironic that the stock photos used in the pamphlet are lacking anyone that looks like her or her family.

It goes on to talk about "taking pride in our product and services" and the importance of "giving the very best to our customers." Finally, it concludes with the company's mission statement: "To enrich the lives of our customers with quality service and quality products."

She sets the pamphlet down and begins to listen to office chatter as more people arrive. Most whisper a silent "hello" to one another, but from what she can tell, conversations don't extend beyond that.

An hour goes by, and Adriana begins to worry that maybe there was a mix-up and she started on the wrong day. Just then, her manager notices her as she walks by.

"Oh, there you are," she says, "We have a cube for you over on the other side. How did you end up over here?"

She can feel her face burn red-hot with embarrassment, "Sorry, I didn't know where to..."

"Never mind that, we have a staff meeting. Follow me," the manager says as she whisks Adriana away toward a conference room.

As Adriana enters the room, she observes something odd. Everyone is standing around the table, lining the room with their backs against the wall. Her manager sits down at the table, followed by a few other people she doesn't recognize. She assumes that the people sitting at the table must be managers or have at least earned the right to sit. Not wanting to presume she's achieved this status yet, she safely retreats to the corner of the room and squeezes herself in with the others lining the wall.

She looks around the room and, while she concedes that maybe it's just Monday, people look tired and despondent.

The meeting begins, and everyone goes around the room to give the group their respective status report. When it comes to Adriana, she nervously introduces herself. Everyone says hello and the meeting moves along.

Her manager then says, "Hey, just as a reminder, we all need to take the diversity training by the end of the week."

Everyone groans.

"I know, I know," she says with a pained look on her face. "Our leadership is just making sure to check the box for the 'politically correct police.'" She makes an "air quote" gesture with her fingers as she rolls her eyes.

Light chuckles are heard around the room. Adriana feels a sinking pit in her stomach.

"How am I supposed to have time for these things?" a man from the other side of the room pipes up. "I've been on the phone all weekend with the team in Germany."

"Work–life balance, right?" her manager replies with a smile on her face.

The group erupts in laughter.

"Sure. Right," the man responds. "Well it turns out that our biggest customer over there is not happy with our new pricing. They're saying that this new pricing model is going to have a huge impact on them."

"That's what they always say when we make these changes," her manager replies. "Don't worry, they'll fall in line. They always do."

He smirks and then replies, "Well, I suppose that would happen if the product they purchased wasn't completely failing."

"That's not our fault," her manager shoots back. "We just sell this stuff, it's not our job to make sure it works." She looks around the room as several people nod in agreement.

Inside Adriana, a growing sense of regret is starting to form. She's beginning to envision lots of late nights and weekends, trying to sell a product that customers hate. She was so excited to work for this company, but now she's getting the dreadful feeling that she's made a huge mistake.

She reflects on the pamphlet she read earlier, and she wonders whether anyone on this team has seen it. She's confident that if she were to ask anyone in the room about the three pillars, they'd probably think she'd lost her mind.

She feels a lump rise in her throat as she begins calculating the steps that would be required to get her old job back.

THE IMPORTANCE OF BELONGING CUES

We've talked about the importance of defining your organization's core purpose and how to script vital behaviors that align with that purpose. However, the third and extremely powerful connector to your culture are belonging cues.

These are the observable behaviors that we see in the everyday interactions of our organizations. They're expressed by what we choose to talk about, what we focus on, and the things we say. They're both verbal and nonverbal, intentional and, many times, unintentional. These cues can be so subtle that we're often unaware how much they are affecting our culture.

In his book *The Culture Code: The Secrets of Highly Successful Groups*, author Daniel Coyle writes that we have used belonging cues to develop cohesion with one another since our earliest ancestors. Our evolution as a species has been highly dependent on our ability to form tribes and work together for common survival. To that end, our brains are hardwired to look for what behaviors are necessary to belong and thrive in a social group. Coyle writes:

> *Belonging cues are behaviors that create safe connection in groups. They include, among others, proximity, eye contact, energy, mimicry, turn taking, attention, body language, vocal pitch, consistency of emphasis, and whether everyone talks to everyone else in the group. Like any language, belonging cues can't be reduced to an isolated moment but rather consist of a steady pulse of interactions within a social relationship.*[10]

---

10 [Coyle] pp. 10–11

Based on the cues she saw on her first day on the job, Adriana safely assumes the team she's joined doesn't put much stock in the company's overall stated values.

We see this discontinuity all the time. The CEO that champions diversity and inclusion, yet the company's board of directors is full of men. A product designer who says that she always "puts the customer first" but pushes back any time the team wants to get early feedback from customers on her design ideas.

What you talk about, what you focus on, and what you nonverbally communicate all send signals to your employees of what you value. We are biologically and psychologically wired to look for these signals. As soon as we observe these signals, we are susceptible to adopting those behaviors and eventually those values.

Doctors Tanya Chartrand and John Bargh call this the *Chameleon Effect*: it's our propensity to adopt the behaviors and attitudes of those around us. In their research, the mere perception of another's behavior automatically increases the likelihood of engaging in that behavior oneself.

Some behaviors seem inconsequential: inside jokes, acronyms, office pranks, and water cooler talk are all ways that we unintentionally signal to others what it means to be part of our "tribe." Yet, the content of those interactions can be incredibly powerful, especially to those who are new to the group and are foraging for ways to demonstrate that they belong.[11]

In fact, scientists believe that this type of mimicry is so essential to our survival that we have developed *mirror neurons*, located in various regions of the brain. They're pathways that cause us to copy one another.

In the book *The Best Place to Work: The Art and Science of Creating an Extraordinary Workplace*, Dr. Ron Friedman illustrates how these social norms come into play:

> *Consider the last time you rode an elevator with a group of strangers. If you're like most people, you entered quietly, moved to a location maximizing the amount of space between you and your fellow passengers, and faced the front to watch the floor numbers change. No one provided you with explicit instructions on how to behave, and you certainly didn't need to wait for your mirror neurons to kick in to tell you what to do.[12]*

These mirror neurons activate instinctively and unconsciously. Over time, we adopt the behaviors and attitudes of those around us. Eventually, we might end up wondering to ourselves, "How did I get to be such a downer?" or, "When did I get to be so aggressive?"

---

11 [Chartrand]
12 [Friedman] p. 209

A company's mission or purpose sets the global course, and the vital behaviors script the actions each member should take, but the belonging cues are what determine the real value system.

HOW BELONGING CUES INFLUENCE YOUR ORGANIZATION

Changing a culture requires us to be constantly vigilant about the belonging cues that we and our leaders are sending out into the organization. Of course, for leaders, your belonging cues will speak much louder than any email missive or state-of-the-union address. What you do, what you talk about, and what you spend your time on will far outweigh any other type of communication. As a leader, change agent, or employee, consider your day-to-day interactions and reflect on whether you're exhibiting the proper belonging cues. In the next section, we discuss key moments where you can position these positive belonging cues. Belonging cues don't have to happen organically; they can be scripted, just as we discussed earlier, by scripting vital behaviors.

Although it can be difficult to assess just how much influence a CEO has over their organization, research suggests that there is a correlation between the CEO's personality and how the organization acts. For example, one study of over one hundred CEOs found that the more a company features its CEO on its website and the higher the CEO's salary is than the next-highest paid employee, the greater the chance that the company makes volatile and impulsive business decisions. In short, narcissistic and ego-driven leaders have companies that are full of narcissistic and ego-driven employees. Likewise, warm and trusting CEOs have more cohesive senior leaders, and intellectually curious CEOs have teams that are more flexible and tolerant of risk.[13]

For individuals who are not in a leadership position, it's important to be aware of how susceptible we are to adopting behaviors and attitudes. If you don't want to work in a culture that delights in gossip, you must resist the urge to engage in it. If you want to encourage your company's desire to create a more diverse and inclusive workforce, you must make demonstrated efforts to include others in the decision making of your workgroup.

In DevDiv, we make concerted efforts to demonstrate, through belonging cues, exactly what our cultural values look like. For example, the Customer-Driven Workshop, we discussed earlier has proven to be a great environment to demonstrate our belonging cues. During the workshop we're mindful of participants' anxiety. For many of them, they've been on the job for only a few weeks.

That's why we craft every experience in the workshop to celebrate when a hypothesis has been proven wrong or when a team realizes that it must pivot on its approach. When partici-

---

13 [Friedman] pp. 212–214

pants see us frame these adjustments as a new discovery to be celebrated, they're seeing us model that learning is valuable in DevDiv.

For instance, during one of our workshops, two groups from completely different parts of the company realized that they were talking to similar customers. They decided that they could increase their overall learning if they combined forces.

As facilitators, we celebrated these two teams and used them as an example for the rest of the group of just how much more powerful our company would be if we all were willing to engage in similar behaviors every day. Shortly thereafter, other teams in the workshop started wandering the room looking for inspiration in one another's work.

As you reflect on the purpose of your organization and the vital behaviors you want to see, think about the subtle cues you send each day. Are there situations in which your comments or behaviors are not aligned with your company's values? How might these behaviors be affecting those around you?

Take Advantage of Key Moments

In the last section, we looked at Adriana's challenging first day on the sales team of a large organization. The first day of work is an incredible opportunity for an organization to impress what they value on new employees. Yet they're often reduced to menial tasks like getting your email working or getting access to applications and files. Little thought is given to creating a lasting impression that will stay with the employee forever.

In *The Power of Moments*, the authors suggest that our lives are defined in moments, typically in the form of the following:

Transitions
> Graduating college, starting a new job, kicking off a new project, reorganization of a division

Milestones
> Getting married, purchasing your first home, retirement

Pits
> Getting laid off, losing an important client, failing a midterm exam

These moments can have a powerful effect on the trajectories of new behaviors or resolve.

However, so many organizations are ambivalent to these moments. They don't wholeheartedly invest in things like first-day experiences, morale events, team bonding, or retirement parties. They're seen as superfluous, time consuming, and costly.

Yet, it doesn't take a lot of resources or even money to invest in these experiences.

Contrast Adriana's first-day experience to the real-life, first-day experience at John Deere, an American corporation that manufactures tractors and other farming equipment. In *The Power of Moments*, the authors detail what it's like on your first day at the company:[14]

> *Shortly after you accept the offer letter from John Deere, you get an email from a John Deere Friend. Let's call her Anika. She introduces herself and shares some of the basics, where to park, what the dress norms are, and so forth. She also tells you that she'll be waiting to greet you in the lobby at 9 A.M. on your first day.*
>
> *When your first day comes, you park in the right place and make your way to the lobby, and there's Anika! You recognize her from her photo. She points to the flat-screen monitor in the lobby—it features a giant headline: "Welcome, Arjun!"*
>
> *Anika shows you to your cubicle. There's a six-foot-tall banner set up next to it–it rises above the cubes to alert people that there's a new hire. People stop by over the course of the day to say hello to you.*
>
> *As you get settled, you notice the background image on your monitor. It's a gorgeous shot of John Deere equipment on a farm at sunset, and the copy says, "Welcome to the most important work you'll ever do."*
>
> *You notice you've already received your first email.*
>
> *It's from Sam Allen, the CEO of John Deere. In a short video, he talks a little bit about the company's mission: "to provide the food, shelter, and infrastructure that will be needed by the world's growing population." He closes by saying, "Enjoy your first day, and I hope you'll enjoy a long, successful, fulfilling career as part of the John Deere team."*
>
> *Now you notice there's a gift on your desk. It's a stainless-steel replica of John Deere's original "self-polishing plow," created in 1837. An accompanying card explains why farmers loved it.*
>
> *At midday, Anika collects you for a lunch off-site with a small group. They ask about your background and tell you about some of the projects they're working on. Later in the day, the department manager (your boss's boss) comes over and makes plans to have lunch with you the next week.*
>
> *You leave the office that day thinking, I belong here. The work we're doing matters. And I matter to them.*

---

14 [Heath-2] pp. 20–21

Wow.

What John Deere has created with their "First Day Experience" is a powerful moment of connection and belonging. Employees who encounter that experience have a sense of the mission and values of the company, not because they read it in a pamphlet, but because they were demonstrated in all the belonging cues sent by employees and management.

This wasn't done by happenstance or luck. The team at John Deere *engineers* these moments. It is in all the little touches and coordination. For example, by ensuring that you have a "John Deere Friend" helping you navigate your first day, even before you arrive. The welcome signs in the lobby and above your cubicle not only make you feel special, but are also reminders to the rest of the employees of their responsibility to stop by and introduce themselves. They script the vital behaviors that are required when a new employee joins the team.

As agents of culture change, you must recognize the power of belonging cues and make certain that we're not inadvertently sending mixed messages to your employees. You must also be on the constant lookout for moments for which you can script belonging cues.

AN EXAMPLE OF HOW DEVDIV SCRIPTS BELONGING CUES

An example of this was our "PM All Hands" event in DevDiv. This is an internal meeting that brings together all our program managers in DevDiv. I was asked if there were any stories we could highlight or topics we could discuss to fill an available time slot in the schedule.

After reviewing the other presentations that were on the agenda, I pointed out that all of them were demonstrating new or upcoming features in the product. There was nothing inherently wrong with that; the All Hands is a great way to get a sense of what everyone is working on. However, it was also a missed opportunity.

"We're an organization that is all about learning," I said. "But we're not showcasing any stories here where someone did something innovative to *learn*."

I explained that, if we were only going to bring program managers up on stage who shipped something, everyone in the audience would wisely assume the quickest way to get equal visibility would be to ship something as well. Keep this going and you'd have an organization motivated to get something shipped, regardless of whether customers want it.

After that realization, we looked across the organization for an exceptional example of learning. Thankfully, we had plenty to choose from and landed on a great example. We decided to feature a junior-level program manager who had discovered new ways to get in contact with our customers. What made the story great was that he had discovered an issue (through our telemetry) that suggested our customers were having trouble deploying a specific application type to Azure, Microsoft's cloud infrastructure offering. Rather than just sending the discovery over to the Azure team, he decided to conduct a quick round of interviews with some of these customers and learned how the deployment issue was affecting them. After talking directly with these customers, he was able to gain a better picture of the issue and could better relate those experiences to the product team and ultimately improve the experience for those customers. What he was able to demonstrate, through his own story, was the willingness to be curious and learn, even though the issue he uncovered wasn't directly tied to his product team's responsibilities. He could've easily said, "Yeah, this issue isn't my problem. This is another team." Instead, he decided to connect with our customers and learn how he might be able to help them.

Allowing this enterprising program manager to take the stage and share his story was a way for us to communicate a strong belonging cue to other employees: *there are many ways to gain recognition in DevDiv. Shipping features our customers love is one way, but so is finding innovative ways to connect with and gather feedback from them.*

It not only gave us a chance to celebrate this employee's unique contribution, it allowed us to signal to everyone else what it takes to become a leader within the organization. Since then, we've become far more mindful of these belonging cues, especially during large events and quarterly staff meetings. We're using these stories to get others to mimic the vital behaviors. It has now become the norm to highlight examples of innovative learning in our All Hands meetings.

What you shine a spotlight on, who you reward and give visibility to, and which outcomes you choose to celebrate are all incredibly powerful ways to build new leaders that will ultimately build your culture.

So when you have an opportunity to shine a light on someone's work, consider the following:

- Why is the work being chosen? Do the reasons align with your cultural values?
- Is there diversity in your selection process? Are you always showcasing the same employees, or are there opportunities to share new faces and voices?
- Do you have a platform in place to adequately celebrate innovative or groundbreaking work?
- How do you typically send out these examples? Is it over email, video, or live presentations? Are your employees engaging with these messages or ignoring them?

Also consider this:

- How are you taking advantage of key moments throughout your employees' careers to reinforce your company's values?
- What's the experience like for a new member joining your company or team? Have you asked them?

- What's the experience like for a member who's leaving the team? Are they acknowledged, or is their departure met with silence and tension?

Building leaders is an essential function for any organization to maintain longevity. Spend time reflecting on the ways you build leaders in your organization. Are your cultural change initiatives including opportunities to raise the visibility and career capital of those who are investing in the new culture?

Rethinking How We Interview New Candidates

As we began to shift our culture to emphasize our learning-first mindset, it became clear to us that the way we were searching for new candidates needed to change as well. John Montgomery, corporate vice president and head of program management in DevDiv, decided to assemble a team to explore how we might reveal skills in potential candidates that reflected learning, questioning, and a willingness to connect with customers.

Throughout their exploration, the team landed on three major epiphanies.

EPIPHANY 1: OUR INTERVIEW QUESTIONS DIDN'T REFLECT OUR VALUES

We discovered that our questions tended to trend toward assessing a candidate's ability to apply existing knowledge and relate it to, in some cases, irrelevant situations.

"I started at Microsoft when we were still asking questions about why manhole covers were round, how many ping-pong balls would fill a 747, and how to reverse a linked list," John remembers. "In 20 years here, I've yet to have to write the code to reverse a linked list or fill a 747 with any kind of ball."[15]

Even though DevDiv had moved on beyond asking those types of questions, we found that our interviews were overly focused on assessing a candidate's existing knowledge. Domain expertise and technical competency are important, but we were unsatisfied because it didn't give us the complete picture.

When Satya visited DevDiv, I'll never forget something he said to us: "People think I hire them because of what they know. Sure, I do. But I also hire people for their capacity to *learn*."

EPIPHANY 2: NOT EVERYONE DOES THEIR BEST WORK IN FAST-PACED, HIGH-PRESSURE SITUATIONS

As the company committed itself to creating a more inclusive environment, we had to admit that the interview process overemphasized a candidate's ability to "think fast" or come up with a solution to a difficult question on the fly. This simply didn't reflect how we worked in DevDiv. We were thoughtful decision makers who welcomed debate and collaboration. Having the

---

15 [Montgomery-2]

"right answer" all on your own, in a matter of minutes, just didn't reflect the reality of how we did our work.

EPIPHANY 3: THE BEST WAY TO SEE HOW SOMEONE WORKS IS TO WORK WITH THEM

During our exploration, John met with a couple of engineering teams and learned that they were beginning to work with candidates to solve a bug or feature as part of the interview process. This was producing promising results, and it felt more collaborative and open. It also gave the candidate an ability to envision what it was like to work with *us*.

Armed with these learnings, John wrote an email with his findings and shared it more broadly with our teams. He asked for feedback and asked for us to pilot new ways of conducting the interview process. We started small, experimenting with different approaches in our interviews, eventually creating the "alternative interview framework" for our program managers.

Here are some of the things we began doing differently:

Sharing the interview in advance

A few days before the interview, we give candidates a detailed outline for the day, including the problem we'll be asking them to work on with us. This gives them time to process our goals and even do a little research on the topic beforehand.

Work on a real problem

We now give candidates problems that are closer to the types of challenges they'll get in their everyday work. The goal isn't to get "free ideas" from potential candidates. It's to give them a clear picture of what the job entails, and it gives us a chance to assess their performance within the context of the real challenges we will assign to them.

Give access to data

In DevDiv, we make decisions based on what we learn from our customers. This requires our teams to have access to data and research. Therefore, during the interview, we will often supply a candidate with customer development research, interview notes, usage data, designs, mockups, or whatever relevant data we have regarding the problem we've assigned to them. It gives the candidate a chance to make informed decisions and gives us insight into their willingness to learn new information before solving problems.

Make it interactive

Question-and-answer interviews aren't how we work with one another in DevDiv, so we don't want that to be the only way we look for candidates, either. Getting "in the trenches" and working together is really the best way to get to know someone. Toward that end, we create moments during the interview for those types of interactions to occur.

Follow a single scenario

To avoid overloading the candidate, we focus their attention on a single scenario or problem space. Throughout the day, our teams take a candidate through understanding the customer and the problem, ideating on a concept, discussing how we might bring the solution to the customer, and strategizing how we can continue to learn after its release. The day ends up being a microjourney of an entire PM project.

Pair interviewers

We found that having two people interview the candidate at a time creates a more dynamic environment, with multiple collaborators. It also helps us by having two sets of ears on our end to ensure that we are listening to candidates closely. Additionally, by pairing interviewers together, we create opportunities to help train future interviewers and diversify our network of available employees to interview future candidates.

Hold feedback until the end

We ask our interviewers to hold their feedback until the completion of the entire process. This helps us avoid biasing one another before we all have had a chance to spend time with the candidate.

At the end of each interview loop, we assess how it went and reflect on our process. We admit that the process is time consuming and it can be difficult to schedule all the necessary employees to interview a candidate for the day, but we've been encouraged by the positive reaction we've had from candidates. In a few cases, candidates whom we eventually hired stated that our interview process was one of the major factors as to why they chose DevDiv over competing offers.

Applying the Hack

Here are some smaller hacks that you can implement to build the next wave of leaders who exemplify the customer-driven culture you're trying to build:

- Create a list of individuals who exemplify a customer-driven culture. Have a manager or leader from your team send each of them a small thank you note to show appreciation for their hard work. John Montgomery routinely sends handwritten thank you notes when someone has gone above and beyond for a customer. Many employees (including myself) treasure these little gestures. A small act of recognition goes a very long way.

- Many times, your organization's leaders need help recognizing others. They have busy schedules and have difficulty seeing the work that's happening on the ground. Give them updates and point to key individuals who are making progress.

- Create opportunities for exceptional employees to have intimate "face time" with your leaders. Scheduling a free lunch for a team and their VP is an easy and low-cost way to shine a spotlight on exceptional behavior.

- If you're in the culture business, you're in the storytelling business. Identify members of your team to act as the "investigative reporters." These people will actively seek out stories that exemplify the new culture. They'll take time to get all the details of the story and create a complete write-up. They can also prepare a set of presentation slides, so that leaders can easily distribute these stories when asked for examples of the new culture.

- Create a platform for others to share their work. At Microsoft, we have a "brown bag" series, in which anyone, from any team, can invite others to bring their lunch and listen to them speak about emerging technology, customer learnings, or new features in the product. These avenues are a great way to highlight exceptional employees in your organization.

- Create a culture room: a section of your team room, lobby, or break room full of pictures, customer testimonials, or stories of employees engaging in vital behaviors. Seeing these stories of success on the walls instead of in their email inboxes can create an energy that breaks the script and literally surrounds employees with the new culture.

- Invest in others. Actively help them achieve their goals and advance in their careers. Delight in their promotions and recognize their achievements. When people feel like you're invested in them, they'll invest in you.

- Town halls, executive Q+As, and divisional meetings are all excellent opportunities to celebrate behaviors that align with your new culture. Reflect on the belonging cues you're sending out during these meetings. Who gets to come up on stage? Who gets the spotlight? Why are they getting the spotlight? Is it because they're exhibiting vital behaviors? If not, consider revising your roster.

Meet Teams Where They Are

Voltaire once wrote, "The best is the enemy of good." Or, put another way, we shouldn't let perfect be the enemy of good enough. This can be so true when we consider how we go about promoting culture change.

I've seen so many change agents become frustrated because they can't influence their teams to change their behavior, but they propose an all-or-nothing approach. You're either all in or all out. The truth is that change can't always be that simple. Product teams will find themselves caught between two cultures: the one that is rooted in the values from before and the one that's being built on new values going forward.

Change is a hero's journey in which we leave the status quo, are confronted with trials and tribulations, and return forever changed by our experiences. It's during these trials and tribulations when our anxiety is highest. It's when we're most likely to doubt our abilities and second-guess our direction.

So if we're in the business of encouraging cultural change, we must realize that we should be in the business of making change less difficult. That requires us to apply the hack of meeting teams where they are.

In this chapter, we discuss the power of pragmatism and how giving over some ground is actually one of the best ways to encourage others to join you. It's not that we should give up our principles or change our cultural vision, but we must understand that we will need to meet people in the context of their current world, not the world as we would like it to be.

Agents of Change: Dr. Wiwat Rojanapithayakorn

In 1993, the Department of Disease Control in Thailand was facing a shocking epidemic. In just three years, new reported cases of HIV infections had climbed by a factor of 10, from 100,000 to a staggering 1,000,000.

Health officials were scrambling to understand the cause. Intravenous drug use and the sharing of needles was part of the cause, but experts believed the growing number of sex workers was the most significant factor. In fact, they believed that 97% of all cases of HIV were linked to sexual transmission from sex workers.[1]

The government was in denial about its growing sex industry and had tried numerous ways to contain it. It tried to address the problem from the "supply side" by cracking down on brothels, but for every brothel the government closed, another popped up. It tried from the "demand side" by going after men and tourists who were flooding the region. That too had little effect.

At the time, Dr. Wiwat Rojanapithayakorn (Dr. Wiwat) was serving as the director of the Office of Communicable Disease Control in Ratchaburi. From his research, Wiwat was convinced that unprotected sex was the most critical behavior that was causing the epidemic. He posited that if they could get 100% condom use within the industry, they would see dramatic results. This was no easy proposition. With the government in denial, it was not looking to find ways to further promote sex work. The thinking was that by instructing the public to engage in safe sex with sex workers, the government would be promoting this illegal behavior.

The numbers were climbing, and Wiwat was horrified to see HIV spreading from community to community. He believed that if they didn't act immediately, Thailand was on the path toward leading the world in HIV infections per capita.

He concluded that the best way to combat the issue was to educate the public and sex workers about the benefits of safe sex. HIV was a behavior-based infection; it was a result of people engaging in behaviors that increased their chance of infection. So he decided to focus his team's efforts on increasing a single vital behavior: condom use.

This was a controversial stance given that many in the public felt that it was putting a small bandage on a severe wound. They believed that it would be far more beneficial and lasting if they could abolish the sex industry altogether. They favored responses that called on society to improve its morals surrounding the issue.

Additionally, men preferred sex without a condom, and brothels were much more willing to provide what their clients wanted over protecting the health and safety of their workers. Wiwat knew that it was an all-or-nothing deal. If only some of the brothels enforced condom use, the other brothels could compete by not using them. For this to work, owners of sex establishments needed to all agree on enforcing condom use. This was also a hard sell because he knew it could be economically damaging to the brothel owners' businesses.[2]

It took courage, but Wiwat and his team pressed forward. They decided they would run an experiment in the Ratchaburi region. They worked with the local police, mayors, and the owners of sex establishments. Their message was simple—they wanted to encourage 100% use of condoms among the sex workers. The vital behavior was scripted: "No condom, no sex."

---

1 [WHO]

2 [WHO]

Condoms were freely distributed, and brothels were asked to make it a requirement that clients used them. Brothels that failed to comply would be shut down by the authorities.

In two short months, the team was shocked by their results. New cases of sexually transmitted infections fell from 13% to 1% in the Ratchaburi region.[3]

Encouraged by the experiment, the team began to roll out the "100% condom use" campaign throughout Thailand. It used an all-out media blitz, playing commercials that promoted safe sex and warned the public about the devastation of AIDS. The team had the commercials running every hour on the nation's 488 radio networks and 6 television networks.

But distributing the condoms and playing advertisements on the radio wouldn't be enough. Wiwat and his team needed to coach sex workers on how to deal with situations in which clients didn't want to use a condom. They trained women who had more experience in the industry, and in turn, those women coached and mentored the younger women. They would role-play various scenarios and practice how to deal with them, getting feedback and refining their approach. Essentially, the team was building leaders within the sex worker community who promoted their protection. These women quickly became influencers and helped younger women advocate for their own safety.

"You must get someone who has done it to teach. I can stand up and teach negotiation skills all day and have no effect," says Mechai Viravaidya, a former politician and activist for family planning and AIDS awareness in Thailand. "If a sex worker is having a difficult time negotiating with a customer, she would go get the more experienced girl to help. Two-on-one negotiations are much simpler."[4]

Compliance with the nationwide program spiked as condom usage rose from less than 25% to more than 90%. Although effecting the change across the entire country took more time than the smaller Ratchaburi region, the team still watched with astonishment as new reported cases of sexually transmitted infections dropped 14% in 5 years and 80% from 1991 to 2001. The World Bank estimates that Wiwat and his team prevented at least 200,000 cases of AIDS in that time period, concluding that it was an "accomplishment that few other countries, if any, have been able to replicate."[5]

What makes Wiwat's example so poignant is his laser-like focus on one vital behavior. When dealing with complex problems, it can be tempting to employ a scattershot approach, trying multiple things and seeing which one sticks. It must have been very difficult for the team to not become swept into trying to help these women in ways that could reduce their dependence on the work in the first place.

---

3 [WHO]

4 [McMillan]

5 [McMillan]

They could've tried to appeal to their moral obligations, shaming them for engaging in such explicit behavior. Instead, they decided to meet the brothel owners and sex workers where they were. Like it or not, these people engaged in the business because it was a way to make money and survive. So they appealed to their economic interests instead. From an economic standpoint, engaging in unprotected sex was simply bad for business. It resulted in the death of workers and time off to treat undesirable infections. It was a difficult but pragmatic decision that ultimately saved thousands of lives.

The Family Health Institute speculates that "perhaps the main reason for the campaign's success was its concentration on a limited objective—the consistent and widespread use of condoms in commercial sex—rather than on wider goals, such as eliminating sex altogether, or the improvement of public morality."[6]

Be Passionately Pragmatic

When bringing about a culture change, results come to those who are willing to be pragmatic and temper their radicalism in favor of making change digestible to those whom they are trying to influence.

This can be incredibly difficult for change agents because they are often the ones who are deeply passionate about and committed to the mission of change. In these cases, they often are their own worst enemy because they begin to resent or demonize those who are not changing quickly enough.

In the early moments of our journey of change in DevDiv, our team had many stumbles as we determined which behaviors we most cared about. It was easy to get specific and prescriptive about the customer-driven behaviors we wanted to see, and when we weren't careful, we were auditors rather than multipliers.

For example, in the early days, we were rigid in our thinking of how the HPF should be used. We had a strong desire to see teams use the hypothesis templates exactly how we designed them.

For instance, the hypothesis template for each stage began with the words "We believe." I remember advocating very strongly that every hypothesis should begin with those words because it would encourage teams to own their assumptions.

Over time, I realized that teams were far more receptive to using the framework when I presented it pragmatically rather than dogmatically. I began to appreciate that the framework worked better when teams embraced it and made it their own. Therefore, I relaxed on the pedantic details and "syntax" of the hypothesis and saw value in focusing teams' attention on the parameters of the hypothesis templates (e.g., [type of customers], [motivation], [job-to-be-

---

done], etc., as shown in Figure 6-1). This made the framework far more approachable and easier to immediately use, regardless of where teams were in their product life cycle.

Customer

We believe [type of customers] are motivated to [motivation] when doing [job-to-be-done]

Figure 6-1. Hypothesis template for the Customer stage with parameters for type of customers, motivation, and job-to-be-done

It became clear to us that program managers and engineers were much stronger at creating lists. We could have them generate far more hypotheses if we focused less on the overall syntax and honed their focus on generating lists full of the various parameters.

So we adjusted our approach and began saying, "The template is a guide to get you started. It's not a requirement that all your hypotheses read like this, but the one thing you want to ensure is that you have at least captured these parameters."

This had a dramatic effect on people's willingness to try our approach. As one colleague remarked, "You've made it deceptively simple. You've broken the bigger task (formulating a hypothesis) into a smaller, more addressable task (creating lists of parameters)."

The value of consistency became less important than the value of adoption. We focused on the things that mattered (the parameters) and less on the things that didn't (the overall syntax).

In DevDiv, I've often joked that we're "passionately pragmatic." We want you to be customer driven, but we want you to *want* to join us, not feel like you were "voluntold" to do things our way. This was a point of view that we grew to appreciate the more we tried to influence teams and met resistance. Just like Wiwat's team, we were tempted to address myriad behaviors, but writing hypotheses was the behavior that unlocked all three of the key vital behaviors: awareness, curiosity, and courage.

By formulating hypotheses, teams generated awareness of their assumptions, which sparked curiosity to experiment and validate or invalidate their hypotheses. It also gave them the courage they needed to accept the data, even if it suggested they needed to pursue a new direction.

It became clear to us that writing hypotheses was the on-ramp to other behaviors: creating discussion guides, talking with customers, and triangulating data by cross-referencing interviews (qualitative) with our telemetry and analytics (quantitative). These behaviors were a result of getting the teams to understand and appreciate the benefits of hypothesis generation and experimentation.

ENCOURAGING PRIDE OF OWNERSHIP

When teams make the process their own, they have pride of ownership and the feeling that they own the direction their team will take. Whichever strategy they employed, the only requirements were that they had hypotheses to communicate what they were trying to learn and that they used customer data to determine whether it was validated or invalidated.

The Customer-Driven Playbook and the HPF both represented an approach that allowed teams the flexibility they needed to make local adjustments, but they also provided a roadmap for how to ensure they remained aligned to the global goal of customer obsession. We gave teams autonomy to make the decision. They couldn't refuse to talk with customers or generate hypotheses, but they didn't need to use the hypotheses templates if they didn't want to.

But, as more and more teams saw people succeeding with the framework, it seemed like a no-brainer to use that approach on their own projects. We didn't mandate its usage or penalize groups that didn't use it. They willingly chose to use it for themselves.

That choice makes all the difference in creating lasting culture change because it gives them the autonomy to chart their own course and the challenge to master a new approach. Autonomy and mastery have both been proven instrumental in creating the motivation that's required to change one's behavior.

Autonomy and Mastery

On June 26, 2014, the New York State Court of Appeals, the highest court in the state, issued a 20-page opinion on a controversial proposal to prohibit the sale of sugary soft drinks in cups larger than 16 ounces (473 ml). The court decided that the proposal "exceeded the scope of its regulatory authority" and effectively killed any hopes that New York City Mayor Michael Bloomberg and his team of health advocates had in reducing soft-drink purchases to fight the obesity epidemic within the city.[7]

Although Bloomberg was disappointed with the ruling, he maintained a brave face and remarked that it was a "temporary setback."[8] As far as his team was concerned, public health was a signature issue. In a four-month time period, the city had lost two thousand residents to diabetes. To them, the ban wasn't a controversial issue, but a necessary evil to prevent a drain on the state's healthcare system and to save countless lives.

Critics were concerned that the proposal contained too many loopholes and exemptions. For example, it wasn't OK for local theaters or restaurants to sell soft drinks larger than 16 ounces, but nationwide chains like 7-Eleven could maintain their "Big Gulp"–branded cups that came in at 64 ounces (1,892 ml). There also wasn't a ban on refills. Additionally, it was unclear

---

7 [Grynbaum]

8 [Ax]

what constituted a "sugary drink." Starbucks, for example, was exempt even though many of their blended coffee drinks contained excessive amounts of sugar. This left local business feeling the burden of competing with one hand tied behind their back. The American Beverage Association took the proposal before the courts, calling the ban "arbitrary and capricious."[9]

Beyond all that, the biggest problem was that many citizens simply weren't in favor of the proposal. Critics started referring to New York as the "nanny state," citing that Bloomberg's proposal suggested residents couldn't make their own choices about the food and beverages they consumed. It treated them like children who had to have their toys taken away because they couldn't be trusted to make the proper decisions.

The opposition from New Yorkers spanned political leanings, race, and gender. According to a study conducted by the *New York Times*, 6 in 10 residents thought the ban was a bad idea. They felt that the ban overreached, infringing on their right to make their own choices, even if those choices were potentially bad for their health.

In our desire to see change happen more quickly, it's tempting to speed things along by applying punitive pressure. However, when we do this, we welcome rebellious confrontation as employees dig in their heels and resist change.

Additionally, mandating or enforcing a behavior change can have unintended consequences. As an example, research has found that schools that engage in a "zero tolerance" policy, indiscriminately suspending students who are involved in fighting, end up disproportionally punishing students of color and students with disabilities.[10]

There's an old saying: "You'll attract more flies with honey than vinegar." And it rings true when you're trying to attract employees to engage in new behaviors. The goal of meeting people where they are is to leave them feeling empowered rather than punished by the new culture.

In his book *Drive: The Surprising Truth About What Motivates Us*, author Daniel Pink outlines the science behind our brains and motivation. If employees feel like they are being compensated fairly and have access to good benefits, it can be difficult to find new ways to motivate them.

However, Pink and many other researchers believe that beyond the essentials, employees want to feel that their work matters, that they have the freedom to apply their own creative thinking to problems, and that they have the ability to create new skills that can help them well into the future. It doesn't cost money to give this to employees. However, it does require patience, flexibility, and a growth mindset from organizational leaders and change agents.

---

9 [Grynbaum-2]

10 [APA]

Just-in-Time Coaching

As we discussed earlier in the book, during our workshops, we create purpose by giving each team a business goal that is relevant to their product area. Other than that, we don't prescribe exactly how they should go about solving that problem. Throughout the week, we slowly introduce tools like the HPF, discussion guides, interviewing techniques, sense-making, and concept-value tests. With each new tool we introduce, we spend very little time giving a lecture and instead try to put the tool in participants' hands as quickly as possible.

Initially, workshop attendees have a strong desire to have you just show them how to complete the task. However, we help them realize that, for our tools to be meaningful and useful, they must try them within their own context.

During one workshop, one of the participants became quite frustrated with me. I had just introduced the notion of using storyboarding to tell the story of an idea. The goal was to give teams time to try storyboarding to express their ideas using a different medium (sketching and storytelling). After briefly explaining the value of storyboarding, I handed out a worksheet for teams to start creating "keyframes" of their stories.

The participant held up the handout, frowned at me and, slightly perturbed, asked, "Can you just tell me what you want us to do?"

"Sure," I replied. "This handout represents three frames of your storyboard. You can fill out these three frames or more if you need them. Use these frames to express what your idea does and how it might impact the customer."

"No, I get that," the participant curtly responded. "I just want you to tell me what this should look like by the time we're finished with this exercise."

"I have no idea," I admitted, "but I'm 100% committed to helping you figure out what it *could* look like."

I decided to reset the conversation. "Why don't you tell me where the team is at in their progress?"

As the participant updated me on the team's progress, it became clear that she was anxious about not getting enough time to complete the previous exercise. They were exploring all the various problems they could solve for the customer, and she felt like there could be more underlying problems. She felt it was too soon to move on to storyboarding ideas because the team needed more time to think about its customers' problems.

I quickly pivoted. "OK. So it looks to me that storyboarding won't be useful right now." I slid the storyboard handout to the side of the table and said, "Let's not use it then. We can use it later, if we think it can help."

We then had a fantastic discussion about the problems the team was exploring and, eventually, those ideas transitioned directly into the storyboarding exercise.

Earlier in my journey as a workshop coach, I would've handled that situation poorly. I would've seen the participant's resistance to the storyboarding exercise as her not appreciating the value of the approach. I would've spent time trying to convince her, feeling pressure to keep the team on task for the next exercise. It would've turned into a battle of wills, and it would've gotten us nowhere. I would've been frustrated, and I would've lost a chance to connect with the team.

I've since learned, through much trial and error, that if I relax my approach, resist getting defensive, and work hard to help others find their own personal value in our tools, it tends to leave us both in a better position, bonded in mutual respect and understanding.

As a coach in our workshops, my job is to put our tools in front of product makers and then work hard to help them find value in those tools as they begin to apply them to their work. I must remain flexible and gently steer teams toward a meaningful direction. Every step of the way, I'm going to check in and ensure the team is getting where it wants to go.

If you're a trainer, facilitator, or coach, you should consider a similar approach.

Feeling stupid or coerced can leave team members feeling diminished. Create room within your programs to give people a sense of freedom and an ability for them to make it their own. Empower them by helping them feel smart and productive, giving them a feeling of ownership and a challenge to master new cultural behaviors.

In the *New York Times* bestselling book *Influencer: The New Science of Leading Change*, the authors write:

> *You must replace judgement with empathy, and lectures with questions. If you do so, you gain influence. The instant you stop trying to impose your agenda on others, you eliminate the fight for control. You end unnecessary battles over whose view of the world is correct.*[11]

Find the Quickest Pathways to Learn

When beginning your journey in building a customer-driven culture, it's easy to be overwhelmed with all the decisions that you need to make and training programs you need to get started. It can be tempting to try to answer all of the questions of how you will scale your initiatives before you even start.

It can be easy to become blocked by another department or your engineering team while you wait for the perfect time to get started engaging your customers. Also, while you're trying to navigate your organization, looking for permission to investigate a new business opportunity or connect with a customer, a small startup with a completely flat org chart is inventing the next disruption to your industry.

---

11 [Influencer] p. 87

One of the questions we get a lot is: "How much data should we collect before we make a decision?" The unfortunate answer is that it depends. We always say collect as much data as you can, as quickly as you can, to make an informed decision on where to go next.

You'll never have perfectly complete data. There will always be gaps, so you do the most learning you can to make your next decision. Determining how comfortable you are with those gaps in knowledge depends on your risk tolerance for a given project. The riskier your decision, the more information you'll require, which in turn will require you to collect more customer data and feedback. Promoting a customer-driven culture isn't about pursuing absolute certainty. It's about de-risking your decisions as quickly as possible by taking advantage of the behaviors and feedback of your customers as strong data points in your decision-making process.

In every decision you make, you want to be asking yourself, "What is the fastest way to test your assumptions regarding this decision?" In his book *The Lean Startup*, author and entrepreneur Eric Ries refers to this rapid learning cadence as the Build, Measure, Learn Feedback Loop. Essentially, it starts with a "leap of faith" or an assumption. You formulate that into a hypothesis, run a lightweight experiment, analyze the results, and then iterate on your idea based on what you've learned.

Although his book envisioned the feedback for fast-moving startups, we've found that the same Lean methods work irrespective of company or workgroup size. The goal is removing waste and bureaucracy in your processes, regardless of whether you're doing foundational or directional research.[12]

For example, if you're trying to determine where a button should be placed in your application (directional research), you'll want to run small, self-contained experiments that are intended to answer that very specific question. Things like usability studies with a small collection of participants or A/B testing within your products can be ways to achieve this.

Conversely, foundational research is required when you're trying to learn about customer trends, motivations, unmet needs, and other wide-ranging details from your customers. Typically, these learnings can come from direct customer interviews, site visits, or focus groups. These can take more time and planning compared to directional research.

However, if your team is engaging in both types of learning, in parallel, you can move much more quickly. For example, if you're bringing in customers for a usability study, it's also a great opportunity to have a brief conversation about the problem space and the various tasks they engage in and to ask them about their motivations and frustrations. Breaking down your research goals and optimizing them for the quickest pathway to learning allows you to create a plan that extracts the most out of your time with each customer you engage with.

---

12 [Ralph]

As a change agent, it's your job to remove any barriers that prevent people from learning and growing. Being rigid and putting up safeguards or barriers that prevent teams from accessing the data they need can be a surefire way to hinder any change effort.

You should look over your org chart. Are there departments or policies that create roadblocks for product teams to access their customers? If a member from a product team wanted to talk to five customers within their target demographic, how long would it take? Hours, days, weeks?

You certainly don't want to bombard your customer accounts with a mountain of inquiries from your product teams; it's understandable that you might want to put a buffer there. However, that buffer shouldn't come at the cost of your product team's ability to connect with and learn from its customers. You'll need to seek the appropriate balance that fits your organization and your customers. Our experience is that customers genuinely appreciate being asked for their feedback. If you're making a product for them that they rely on, typically they have a vested interest in helping make it better. If you're finding it difficult to locate customers who are willing to talk with you, you might need to consider creating gratuity programs that give customers an incentive to make time in their busy schedules to connect with you. It doesn't always need to be in the form of monetary compensation, although that does help. You can offer additional product support, discounts on additional features or accessories, or early access to the next version of your product.

You can also consider a program in which account managers connect the customer to the product team in a structured setting. Getting your sales or accounts teams involved in creating your feedback loop not only takes advantage of the strong customer relationships your sales teams have created, but it's also a great way to get your product and sales teams to regularly collaborate.

Empathize with Your Enemies

As we seek culture change within our organizations, we will be met with countless obstacles, political maneuvering, and perhaps even inaccurate claims about our true motives. Successful change agents see these obstacles as opportunities to find common ground. The following true story is an example of this.

AGENTS OF CHANGE: VOLPI FOODS

In 1898 John Volpi traveled from his home in Milan, Italy, to the shores of America, bringing with him a centuries-old European tradition of dry-curing meats. His vision was to start his business by offering handcrafted dried meats to residents and families.

In 1902, he opened Volpi Foods in a small St. Louis neighborhood known as The Hill. He offered dried salami that was small enough to fit in the pockets of the local clay miners. The product was a hit, and Volpi's business became a mainstay in St. Louis.

Today, Volpi Foods has been in operation for more than a century, distributing its hand-crafted Italian meats in grocery stores throughout the United States. Lorenza Pasetti, John's great-niece, eventually became the president of Volpi Foods, continuing the family tradition.

One year, while away at a foods show, Pasetti received a frantic phone call from a staff member back at the St. Louis office. According to the employee, they had just received a copy of a letter that had just been sent to Costco, one of Volpi's biggest retail customers. The letter was from a US attorney representing the powerful Consorzio del Prosciutto di Parma, one of Italy's global enforcers of food trademarks.

Essentially, the Consorzio claimed that Volpi was violating the law through its use of words like "traditional" and "prosciutto" on its labels. The organization believed that Volpi was not using traditional methods, which triggered an investigation from the US Department of Agriculture (USDA). For a company that prided itself on its reputation for maintaining its traditions and handcrafted quality, these charges were devastating.

"The letter denounced our prosciutto product and charged Volpi with infringement of US label law," Pasetti explains. "This situation was nothing short of a crisis—and it attacked Volpi's reputation, one we had built over a century."[13]

If it was determined that the Consorzio's claims were true, Volpi would be forced to remove words like "Italian" and "Proscuitto" from its packaging. This would require Volpi to abandon its entire identity, leaving it unable to compete with the growing US demand for specialty and authentic meats from Italy. The company's future would be doomed under these restrictions.

Pasetti was at a loss for what to do next. The company was doing well, but it wouldn't be able to sustain the cost of a long legal battle. After contacting the USDA, she found that the agency was starting to backtrack on its previous clearances of the company. Costco was concerned that it might face a class action lawsuit for carrying products that mislead consumers regarding their authenticity and thus was considering removing all Volpi products from its shelves. Things were unraveling quickly.

Pasetti decided to take a moment and consider the situation. She needed to understand where the Consorzio was coming from. Rather than remain incredulous to the claims that their products were inauthentic, she decided to research the Consorzio's position.

She went online and learned that the Consorzio's mission was to ensure that when companies labeled their products with words like "Italian" that they were adhering to the traditional Italian style of food making. Although she believed the Consorzio had unfairly targeted her company, Pasetti could still empathize with its mission. She agreed that, if anyone could claim their products were made with traditional Italian methods, it would diminish the reputation of the craft. In the end, the Consorzio was trying to maintain the quality of Italian traditions; this

---

13 [Hansen] p. 132

was a good thing for the entire industry. For companies like Volpi, putting the word "Italian" on its products was a source of profound pride. The Consorzio was working hard to ensure that it stayed that way.

Armed with this insight, Pasetti decided to set up a meeting with the Consorzio. She believed that if she could get in front of them and tell the story of her great-uncle's company, they would realize that Volpi valued Italy's traditions just as much as they did.

That summer, Pasetti found herself in front of the Consorzio in the northern Italian city of Parma. Sitting across from her were two Italian businessmen, twice her age. Through the meeting, she told them about Volpi's heritage, how John, her great-uncle, had a dream of bringing the best of Italy to American families. She walked them through their process, spending time and detail on how they prepared their meats at scale, but still adhered to the Italian traditions and craftsmanship. Because Pasetti understood and deeply empathized with the Consorzio's mission, she was able to meet them where they were. She could speak to their values and show them that they were partners, not enemies. She helped them realize they shared a common language and a common passion for the quality and precision of traditional methods.

The meeting worked, the two men were convinced, and the Consorzio retracted all of its claims.

By taking a moment to consider the Consorzio's position and truly empathizing with it, Pasetti was able to speak to the representatives in a way that showed she understood and valued what it was trying to do. Through empathy and understanding, she avoided years of costly court battles. She might have been justified in fighting back, but the approach of seeking understanding and a commitment to meet the Consorzio on their claims and positions proved to be the best course of action.

Melting the "Frozen Middle"

When pursuing a culture that is focused on the customer, it's a mistake to assume businesses will shift their processes because it's the right thing to do for the customer. As teams resist change, you must keep emotions in check and resist the urge to demonize people who reject your proposals. All too often, change efforts fail because change agents find themselves embattled in an "us versus them" conflict. It becomes a battle of wills rather than a collaboration to improve processes on behalf of customers.

As the person or group that is proposing the change, you have complete control over the discourse. How you respond to your detractors is an important indicator to everyone for how you plan to lead the effort. Demonstrating empathy and a desire to seek understanding can go a long way toward thawing tensions, and it's a great way to model to others your new cultural values. These challenges can often be the most important opportunities for us to demonstrate what we want the new culture to look like. If you're promoting a culture that highlights the need for employees to empathize, learn, and understand customer needs, it would be an ironic misstep if your change team wasn't demonstrating that behavior when encountering employee concerns.

Many change efforts will find the most detractors within middle management. Depending on your organization, these are team leads that are leery to "rock the boat" or to make radical changes in how things are done. They can be considered the "frozen middle"; effectively, your senior leadership wants change, your employees want change, but the managers between those two groups resist.

This phenomenon is known as the *middle-status conformity effect*. Social scientists have long posited that this happens because the layer of middle management has the most to lose.

Middle managers can be insecure about sweeping changes in process because they finally have standing within their groups. In a sense, if you're a lower-level employee and you make a mistake, you might fall from low to lower. If you're a senior-level director, you have some distance from on-the-ground decision making. If you're a middle manager, a mistake can be devastating. As a middle manager, there's an intense pressure to prove to your directors and your reports that you have everything under control. Any misstep can be interpreted as an inability to lead. As sociologist George Homans observed, "Middle-status conservatism reflects the anxiety experienced by one who aspires to a social station but fears disenfranchisement."[14]

Depending on the type of change you're asking for, what might seem like a small change to you can seem like an incredibly risky change to a manager who is responsible for a team. In most cases, they're the most exposed if the change doesn't produce the desired results.

Therefore, it's best to operate by making the charitable assumption whenever possible. Take time to empathize with your managers, leads, or any other detractors. Seek to understand their underlying concerns regardless of whether you believe they're unfounded or misguided. Showing that you care about their concerns and that you're not just going to dismiss them will go a long way toward building their trust.

Let's be clear: working with people who oppose you is difficult. These battles can become volatile or even downright petty. Change is hard, and it can bring out the worst in us, especially when you've been successful doing things the old way.

In the book *Rebels at Work: A Handbook for Leading Change from Within*, authors Lois Kelly and Carmen Medina (whom we highlighted in Chapter 3) suggest that when you find yourself angry or frustrated, you must look at the other side:

Try to understand what it's like to be the person (or group) you're angry with. What are they trying to protect? What makes them uncomfortable? What are they afraid of? How people talk about something conveys more information than the words themselves. Lis-

---

14 [Grant] p. 83

ten for emotion beneath the words. This empathy will help neutralize your anger and help you see more clearly.[15]

Use Their Energy and Push for Positivity

Perhaps you're in a situation in which you need to give constructive feedback to the person or group that is affecting the team's ability to change to the new culture. Maybe it's an employee who refuses to make time to talk with customers and creates friction any time the team wants to show customers early work to get feedback.

In those situations, it might require you to have a direct conversation with them and ask for the behavior to be corrected.

Microsoft has an online tool called Perspectives where employees can write about your performance and submit it to you and your manager for review. Amazon has its Anytime Feedback Tool with which employees can anonymously submit employee feedback.

Although, for the most part, these are great tools to help individuals understand how their behaviors affect those around them, this type of feedback isn't always conducive to learning. Pointing out an employee's lack of performance can be diminishing, especially if we don't have a window into the complete picture. Dishing out negative criticism isn't "just being honest"; it's an ineffective way to encourage someone to change their behavior.

Studies show that giving people negative feedback on their performance doesn't encourage them to reflect and change; often, it discourages learning.[16] The challenge with feedback tools is that humans are not very good at rating other humans. Research shows that we fall victim to our own subjectivity, and it's difficult for us to provide a stable definition of an abstract quality such as the effectiveness of a presentation or whether someone understands the business. Our rating is influenced by our personal biases and preferences. It can also be influenced by past experiences, our current standing within the organization, or our own personal goals. The bottom line is that the only thing that we're truly qualified to give feedback on is how someone's behavior affects our own personal feelings and experiences.

It turns out that focusing on our shortcomings is not the best way to encourage a culture of learning. In fact, studies show that when you give someone feedback on where they are failing, it ignites the "fight or flight" response, effectively shutting down their ability to listen and process what you're telling them. In effect, receiving negative feedback impairs our ability to learn.

---

15 [Kelly] p. 76

16 [Buckingham]

Think back to the last time someone told you that they were unhappy with something you did. Your pulse quickens and your mind fires as you try to come up with a reasonable explanation for your behavior.

Educators, particularly those of children, have known this for years. Positive reinforcement —focusing and pointing out behaviors that we want to see more of—is a far better mechanism for giving feedback than constantly pointing out where a student is failing.

Consider two different ways in which a teacher might give feedback to children in her class. First, using a method that focuses on the behavior that needs to be corrected:

> *"Jackie, you need to share with others."*
>
> *"Shari, your desk is a mess."*
>
> *"William, you need to do a better job during group time."*

Contrast that with focusing on the behavior that should be repeated:

> *"Jackie, I really like how you're sharing with Molly."*
>
> *"Shari, thank you for putting your books in your desk before leaving for recess."*
>
> *"William, I like how you and Justin were working together during group time."*

Pointing out excellence rather than failure requires a mindset change, but it can be a powerful tool when encouraging behavior change.

Maximum learning happens when you focus on people's competencies: when you start the conversation with what they're doing right. You build trust, and you'll find that people will be more receptive when pointing at ways that they can improve their performance even more.

If you're considering leveling someone with negative feedback, take a moment to reflect on any positive behaviors that you can use and build on top of.

REDIRECTING BEHAVIOR

For example, let's imagine that you're working with a software team that's exploring the problem space of families traveling on flights with children. It's unclear what problems, if any, exist for these customers. The team is just getting started in looking for the best problems to solve to drive the biggest impact.

James, a software developer on the team, already has an idea for a mobile app and wants to start coding a prototype. The rest of the team is concerned that if James starts building an app, all of the resources will go toward that idea before they've even validated that a mobile app is the best solution for customers. He's done this with past efforts, and the team has found themselves in the position of having a fully baked solution in search of a problem. They're really concerned that they're heading down a familiar path and are hoping that they can try a customer-driven approach by having discussions with customers—before they start to write code.

During team meetings, James insists that the mobile app is the best way to go and that the team is wasting valuable time by trying to validate the idea with customers. "I could build it faster than it would take for you all to validate if it's the right idea or not," he exclaims. "We should just release a limited version of the app and see how it goes."

It can be tempting to push back on James's desire to release a product without validating the need with customers first. We could point at previous projects for which he's employed this strategy and it did not work. If we're called in as mediators, it can be tempting to side with the team and put James in his place.

Although this might give us a short-term win with the rest of the team, it can prove problematic down the road when we need James to help us develop an idea that has been validated with customers.

In this case, it would be best to channel James's energy to prototype. If we take a moment to reflect, we can empathize with him as he's trying to apply his skillset (i.e., writing code) to help the team under a new customer-driven culture. It's not that he's unwilling to be customer driven, it's that he wants to offer his best skills to the effort, rather than struggle trying to adopt new techniques for interviewing customers.

A better approach would be to tell James that we love his enthusiasm to prototype and point out how prototyping is an excellent way to get feedback from customers. We could advise against completely coding the prototype but encourage more lightweight exploration with customers, such as showing low-fidelity mockups or discussing benefits and limitations of the concept with customers. Rather than fight James on his desire to start prototyping, we're actively choosing to take advantage of his energy and point it in a direction that can be less disruptive to the rest of the team. James will see that we value his contribution to the team and that we're trying to align his skills in a way that can be helpful for where the team is currently at. It's a redirection of his efforts to ensure that it still aligns with our goals of transitioning to a customer-driven organization. Instead of trying to generate new energy around our ideas, we consider James's passion and determine the best way to make use of it.

This isn't giving up your principles or plan, but it's doing the hard work to find alignment between your goals and the goals of the people you're trying to influence. Making that connection is the quickest way to gain their trust, and it further demonstrates the belonging cues of the customer-driven culture you're trying to build—one that is built on learning, inclusivity, and psychological safety.

Make Change Digestible

On September 17, 2011, a group of two hundred protestors gathered in Zuccotti Park in New York's Wall Street financial district. The gathering was organized by a pro-environment group and an anticonsumerist publication, *Adbusters*, that focused on economic equality, greed, and corruption, particularly in the financial services sector.

This protest was only a few short years after the US economy had fallen into the Great Recession. Protesters were frustrated as they watched the US government sign the Emergency Economic Stabilization Act (also referred to as the "bank bailout"). The bill made it possible for the government to spend $700 billion dollars of taxpayer money to purchase toxic assets from failing banks so they could ensure their continued operation.

During the recession, millions of Americans lost their jobs, their homes, and their businesses and still had not seen any economic relief. Many Americans were beginning to feel that the system was stacked against them, and tensions were high. The protesters claimed they represented the "99%," reflecting the opinion that the wealthiest 1% of Americans benefitted the most under the current economy, leaving everyone else with nothing.

The organizers of the protest encouraged attendees to bring tents and supplies as the plan was to "occupy Wall Street" and completely disrupt the day-to-day business of the country's top financial institutions. The idea was that protestors would live outside, in front of banks and other financial buildings, to show the world that they were in crisis. They wouldn't leave until they saw some meaningful reform.

The movement gained the immediate attention of international press, and cameras soon showed several demonstrations taking place in the financial districts of other cities. Thousands of people poured into these areas, sitting and remaining immovable, holding signs and shouting at business professionals as they went into work. Nearly 60% of Americans supported the movement because they felt it perfectly captured their frustration with income inequality.[17]

Yet, two months after the movement began, the protestors in Zuccotti Park were forced to leave. Even though they tried to keep the movement alive by occupying banks, corporate headquarters, board meetings, and college campuses, the movement largely fizzled out as quickly as it began.

How could a movement that had widespread attention and support stop so abruptly?

One theory is that the change was indigestible to mainstream Americans. In a sense, protesters were asking for too much. To participate in the Occupy Wall Street movement, you needed to stop everything you were doing and either fly to New York or travel to your nearest financial district. Once there, you needed to commit to camp out for an undetermined amount

---

17 [Cooper]

of time. This was a tough proposition for many who were either busy looking for work or working multiple jobs to keep families afloat.

TYPES OF RADICALS

In his book *Originals: How Non-Conformists Move the World*, Adam Grant suggests that change movements benefit from "tempered radicals." These are individuals who find ways to get their ideas adopted among the mainstream. They ask for just enough to create meaningful change, but not too much that that they push willing parties away.

This is an incredibly difficult balance. You might find that within your own change effort, there's a spectrum of radicalism. Some individuals find that change isn't happening fast enough. They're frustrated and don't understand why others are dragging their feet. They propose radical ideas that push boundaries and shake up the status quo. On the opposite side of the spectrum, you have tempered radicals. They're not interested in creating unnecessary tension and are highly allergic to change that will create backlash.

Essentially, each party is frustrated with the other because they feel they're either asking for too much or too little. In some cases, each party will point to the other as the reason why change isn't happening.

The reality is that you need *both* personalities in your change effort. Radicals help push the envelope. They keep the foot on the gas pedal, preventing the change team from becoming complacent or resting on past successes. Tempered radicals reel you in, helping you appreciate that "Rome wasn't built in a day." They tend to be far more pragmatic and are willing to meet people where they are. They seek to partner with their detractors and create common bonds that help their ideas go mainstream.

If you have these types of factions in your change movement, the trick is meeting both groups where they are and seeking compromise, letting them know you appreciate the passion or trepidation they bring to the effort. Engage both your radicals and your tempered radicals in meaningful debate, enlisting them both to help you find the proper balance for your change effort.

Additionally, you can utilize each personality when the context demands it. For your more difficult, nonconforming groups, it might be best to send in the tempered radical who will push for meaningful change but do it in a way that is more digestible to a skittish group.

For teams that are convinced of the new culture and are ready to get started, it's best to send in your radicals. They're already working with a group that's converted, so they can push them beyond the boundaries of what they thought was possible.

In our journey in DevDiv, we had to appreciate that not all our software teams were in a place to immediately take advantage of our customer-driven approach. We had to meet each team where they were. Some were ready and able to radically change their working process; others needed more time and a measured approach. The key was having a change effort that supported both desires.

Consider your own customer-driven change effort:

- Are you asking for too much? Too little?
- Are there teams that would benefit from tempered radicalism?
- Are there teams you can push into even more radical areas of change?

Embrace Existing Tools

When promoting a change in culture, I've found that there can be a tendency to create distance from the "old way of doing things." To that end, there can be a strong desire to introduce wide-sweeping systems or tools to encourage new behaviors. I've seen change agents tie their cultural ambitions to the rollout of a tool or software product. It's not that these tools aren't helpful—for example, Microsoft Dynamics is a comprehensive suite of tools that helps organizations all over the world organize their customer data and manage their relationships—however, these tools should not be a means to an end.

Depending on your resources, you might be ill-equipped to encourage culture change *and* engage in a massive software rollout. Therefore, you should consider your strategy wisely and look for smaller wins that can bring about more immediate change.

Working at a software company, there was a plethora of tools that we could've employed to gather and collect all the information that was being generated by our teams as they conducted customer interviews. In a sense, it was difficult to resist the urge to immediately jump to a software solution to use the data in even more complex ways. We're a software engineering company; it's hard not to look at everything as a software engineering problem. However, we quickly realized that software products can't bring about meaningful cultural change. They can only augment it.

We believed that rolling out a massive, centralized database and expecting all our employees to engage in filling out forms and data entry for every conversation they were having was going to create too much friction. It was enough that we were asking them to engage in new behaviors (e.g., formulating hypotheses, creating discussion guides, talking with customers). To ask them to also add extra data-entry behaviors to their workday, especially when those behaviors would not be of immediate value to the employee, was a bridge too far.

However, we also didn't want to lose all the organizational learning that was happening from every customer interview.

So we decided to be far more pragmatic. In DevDiv, we tend to be a pretty email-heavy culture. Email is widely used and adopted. For better or worse, email is our default communication tool.

Rather than try to implement something new and try to force everyone to use it, we decided to take advantage of what was already in place. We created an email alias called "CD Notes" (Customer Development Notes), and it was the de facto email address that all product teams used to share their notes from customer interviews.

Essentially, the ask was simple. When you're sharing notes from your interviews, be sure to add CD Notes to the CC line. This was an extremely easy behavior for teams to adopt.

It also created a spot for anyone on the team to see the latest interviews and learnings. Our leadership team would periodically reply to emails with follow-up questions, suggestions, or further learnings. The minute employees saw that these emails were being read and commented on by leadership, investment in the behavior increased. Additionally, employees used search features already in Microsoft Outlook and Exchange to comb through previous emails and investigate past learnings. The email address became a past record of our customer learnings.

Was this the best solution? No. For instance, new employees couldn't access emails from before they were hired. However, new employees created their own workarounds. For example, they would find an employee who had been with DevDiv longer and ask them to search their email for the things they were interested in. Not perfect, but acceptable.

And that is the key with a lot of this. Being pragmatic in the face of changing behavior is not letting perfect get in the way of good enough.

Microsoft Teams, which is a collaboration tool that uses chat, messaging, video conferencing, and document storage, is another tool that is becoming more widely used. We've leaned into that tool as well to encourage sharing information. For example, when conducting an interview with a customer remotely, the team will chat in real time, discussing the customer feedback and reacting to what it's learning.

However, if a team wants to use Slack (a direct competitor to Microsoft Teams), we don't push the issue. The team has already invested in the tool and has found a way to incorporate it into its day-to-day workflow. It would take too much time to uproot that behavior, and we'd spend more time trying to influence tool use over the more vital behavior: connecting with customers.

As you push for a change in behavior, consider how you might use lightweight tools that are already in use. Resist the urge to reduce cultural change to be about compliance with software or process adoption. This will prevent your team from becoming embroiled in unnecessary battles that miss the larger mission of creating less distance between product teams and their customers.

If you must introduce new tools, processes, or software products, try to implement them in ways that reduce the burden on employees. Gather feedback about the implementation and be willing to make concessions if it means that you'll reduce unnecessary friction with teams.

Consider testing new tools in smaller batches. Run a pilot with a small team and work out the kinks before rolling them out more broadly.

Meet Your Customers Where They Are

One final point. In this chapter, we've focused exclusively on how you should meet your fellow employees where they are regarding your culture change efforts. This requires us to find ways that make change more digestible to them. We're consistently finding a balance of challenging them to change outdated behaviors but not pushing so hard that it causes backlash or revolt.

This same hack should be applied to your customers as well. Any change-management effort, whether you're changing the culture of your organization or trying to change the way customers interact with your products, requires patience, reflection, and empathy.

It requires that we seek to understand where our customers are coming from, where their pain points are, and how the changes we introduce in our products affect them.

In Chapter 3, we talked about how when you're applying the hack of "Building Bridges, Not Walls," you're effectively improving both sides of the glass. You're improving the relationships and interactions of your product teams with one another so that you can improve the relationships and interactions of those teams with their customers.

If you're rolling out a new pricing structure, deprecating a beloved feature for a better alternative, or pushing customers to a new ecosystem, it's vitally important that you deliver the correct balance of change. You'll discover this balance by engaging with your customers and having meaningful conversations with them. Uncovering their motivations and goals—the things they want to achieve with your products—will help guide you when you're trying to shift your product offerings. When working with your customers in a consistent and continuous way, you're always in step with them, so you have a deeper understanding of how changes in offerings will affect them.

Change can be difficult for your fellow employees, but make no mistake: it can be equally or more difficult for your customers. As you find successful ways to win over your detractors, make note of those strategies. These strategies can prove useful for influencing customers to change as well.

Applying the Hack

Here are some ideas that you can use to encourage learning over knowing in your teams and throughout your organization:

- Spend quality time with the product team you're trying to influence first. Attend their standups and, if possible, meet with their leadership team. Understand their values and business goals. By asking questions, listening, and observing behaviors, you can uncover their motivations and unmet needs. These can be applied when influencing them to change their process or engage more with customers. Interweaving their goals and the language they use to express those goals will show them that you're invested and that you appreciate their unique needs.

- Avoid solutions that are "one size fits all." You need flexibility in your approach that allows others to feel like they own their own process.

- Pick and choose your battles carefully. For example, if a team member wants to call a customer interview "an interview" and not "an experiment," it's probably best to let them have that win. The goal is to encourage terms that exemplify a language of learning. If employees are offering alternatives to the terms you're suggesting, use it as a point of building, rather than tearing down. Although sharing the same language is vitally important, it shouldn't be pursued dogmatically.

- Actively work to eliminate your own hubris. Starting with a group by demanding change, holding on to dogmatic principles, or demonizing outdated behavior is the quickest way to be ignored. Avoid being the "company's auditor," as teams will be leery to work with you if they feel that you're there to scold or correct their behavior.

- Just as you want others to empathize with your customers, consider generating empathy for your teams. Avoid the fundamental attribution error. This is the bias that presumes a person's behavior is a result of an internal factor (e.g., personality) rather than an external factor (e.g., environment). When a team is resisting change, don't demonize them—actively seek to understand why. Even when someone appears to be difficult or obstructive, try to make the charitable assumption and understand that it may have nothing to do with you, your team, or your change effort.

- Be open to new ideas or optimizations on your approach. Don't put pressure on yourself to get everything "standardized" and "consistent." Where appropriate, let teams have ownership over the process and allow them to make it their own.

- Before preparing a request of another team member or division, ask yourself, "What could *they* use help with?" Offering help with their goals can demonstrate that you're interested in developing a mutually beneficial relationship. Offering help, without immediately asking for something in return, goes a long way in developing long-term trust and support with others.

- In meetings, rather than waiting for your turn to speak or present your part, be mindful of other discussions that are happening. Sometimes, we fall into a pattern of thinking to ourselves, "This conversation doesn't apply to the work I'm doing, so I'm going to check my email" during meetings. When we do this, we miss an opportunity to ask ourselves how this conversation might apply to the work we're doing. Learning about what others care about can be a powerful way to align our work to the goals of others on our team.

- Rather than spend 100% of your time trying to convince the naysayers, consider spending your time supporting those who have joined you in changing the culture. Reflect on your investments using the "80/20" rule (also known as the Pareto Principle). Essentially, 20% of your activities should generate 80% of your results, not the other way around. If working with a team is going to be costly and is likely to produce little impact, consider walking away and returning at a later point.

Make Data Relatable

As teams in DevDiv began employing our customer-driven methods, we found there were times when they would become frustrated by the lack of action in response to their discoveries.

For example, I'd work with a team and they would do a fantastic job of identifying their assumptions, formulating them into hypotheses and running round after round of customer interviews. They were doing all the right things, yet it would be difficult to move the project beyond just data collection. These teams would become frustrated, wondering why their validated or invalidated hypotheses weren't enough to move their teams into action.

If you're an organization that is suffering from low customer satisfaction scores, a decline in product engagement, or customer indifference toward new products and services, these situations can be very urgent. In the face of those issues, it can be incredibly frustrating when you're met with inaction or apathy.

In this chapter, we explore the power of generating data that is relatable. This is an incredible hack that, when applied correctly, can inspire people to change their behavior in positive ways.

We cannot influence change with data and numbers alone. You need stories to bring that data to life in a way that captures people's attention and compels them to action. In a customer-driven culture, your customers' stories are what keep your employees connected to the company's mission. Your customers must become more than a set of numbers in a spreadsheet or a collection of responses in a survey.

The same is true of your employees. Their stories of success inspire us to engage in the new culture. They give us examples of how to belong and what it looks like when we behave under the new values that are being promoted.

Therefore, as change agents, we must become masterful storytellers. We must be able to identify key stories from both the customer side and the employee side. We shape these stories, build upon them, and find interesting ways to share them throughout the organization. By applying this hack, we create a roadmap of examples that eventually leads us to our new culture.

Agents of Change: Rescuing the Wild Boars Football Team

On July 2, 2018, John Volanthen, a British cave diver, had literally reached the end of his line. Submerged in flood waters deep within the recesses of the Chiang Rai cave network in Thailand, his team was using a lead line to help him navigate the 2.5 miles of treacherous terrain. The tether was a literal lifeline, helping him find his way back to the entrance of the cave. As he stared at the end of the rope, he realized this was as far as he could go if he wanted to safely find his way back.

John, his team, and Thailand officials were desperately searching for the Wild Boars youth football team.

Twelve boys, between the ages of 11 and 16, had entered the cave with their coach nearly two weeks prior. What was supposed to be an exciting team adventure, exploring the cave's natural wonders, had turned into a nightmare when a monsoon developed out of nowhere. The rescue team believed that, as the water levels rose, the boys and their coach were forced deeper into the cave to avoid drowning. They feared that without light, food, water, and, most important, breathable air, their chances of survival were grim.

For John, it was becoming increasingly clear that if the rescue team waited any longer, this would cease to be a rescue mission and they would all be forced to accept an unimaginable reality: these children would be lost forever. In that moment of desperation, John did the unthinkable. He took the end of his line reel, stuck it into the mud, and moved forward into the dark cave. If he was going to find these boys, he was going to have to risk traveling without his lifeline.

Thankfully, he didn't have to travel much farther. After moving into the cave another 15 feet (4.6 meters), his light flashed across what looked like a face. He jerked his head back and his headlamp caught the sight of a boy, squinting against the first light he'd seen in days. John immediately began scanning the area. He found another boy, and then another.

His pulse quickened, "How many of you?" he cried out to one of the boys.

"Thirteen," the boy replied, shielding his eyes from the light.

"Brilliant."

He found all of them alive.

Another boy shouted, "Eat, eat, eat."[1] They were starving.

What followed was a harrowing attempt to rescue the boys and their coach. Essentially, the rescue team was left with two options. They could give the boys supplies and have them wait until the water levels dropped, allowing them to walk out of the cave. Surprisingly, this option would require the boys to live in the cave for an unimaginable four months. The rescue team was pumping 1.6 million liters of water out of the cave per hour, but with the monsoon season

---

1 [Suhartono]

approaching, it wouldn't be enough to completely clear out the cave. The chances for illness, injury, or sheer psychological damage were too great. The second option was nearly just as improbable. The team could try to get the boys out.

The plan was audacious, to say the least. They would ask 13 inexperienced divers, who had spent over a week in a dark cave without food or water, to swim a route that had claimed the life of an experienced Navy SEAL. To do this, divers would need to teach the kids how to navigate an extremely difficult scuba dive. Some parts of the cave were so narrow they would be required to take their equipment off to fit through and then reconnect to it on the other side, all while holding their breath, and, one by one, the divers would guide them through the 2.5 miles (4 km) back to their families.

If you turned on any major news network, they were running nonstop coverage of the effort. Experienced divers, ex-military officials, and countless other pundits took to the airwaves to assess and comment on the situation. It seemed like everyone had a theory of whether the boys and their coach would survive. Psychologists were asked about the boys' potential mental state, and Thai officials were interviewed about every detail. At one point, the divers had snaked a camera into the cave so the boys could communicate with their parents. It was an unbelievable moment of celebration and heartbreak. The boys were so close to their parents, yet so far.

The world was captivated. For weeks, there wasn't a channel, newscast, news blog, or newspaper that wasn't covering the story. It had something in it for everyone: a daring escape, an engineering challenge that had engaged the greatest minds, and pride and nationalism as many countries offered their support and resources. For a brief, historic moment, the world was working together, with a common purpose of returning this football team home to their families.

But why?

There are children, just like the boys of the Wild Boars football team, who face dire circumstances every single day. According to CARE, a nonprofit humanitarian effort, measles, malaria, and diarrhea are the three biggest killers of children—all preventable diseases. One in five children lack safe drinking water, and every day almost two thousand children die from diseases related to lack of basic sanitation. More than three hundred million children are starving and are suffering the consequences of long-term malnourishment.

For many, these are alarming and urgent statistics that warrant immediate intervention. Largely, the world remains unmoved. But when 12 young boys' lives were in peril, the world galvanized itself into action.

Now, to be clear, it was phenomenal to see the best minds come together for those boys in Thailand. In fact, divers were able to successfully rescue every single boy and their coach. It was an incredibly historic moment of triumph for their families and the world.

Yet, it remains incredibly difficult to capture the world's devotion to all these other issues that children face every day.

Certainly, the story was sensational, which is why it received so much attention. For children, living in poverty has been a systemic problem for centuries, and we've all been introduced to the problem in one way or another. However, there was something special about this story of the Wild Boars football team beyond the novelty of it. The story had the power to engage the entire world with concern and common purpose. The reason this story had so much power over the public's consciousness wasn't just because it was harrowing and remarkable; it was that it was incredibly relatable.

It didn't take much for a parent watching CNN in Iowa to put themselves in the shoes of one of the distraught parents in Thailand. Looking at the grainy images of those boys, soaking wet and scared, stuck in a dark, narrow pocket of the cave, it was impossible not to imagine our own children in a similar plight. The boys and their coach in Thailand weren't a nameless, faceless statistic. They were relatable; they were ordinary people caught in an extraordinary circumstance. Through news coverage, images, and interviews, we learned their stories and shared in their families' heartache.

Such stories have a profound effect, shifting us to a common goal (in this case, saving the boys and their coach) and inspiring us into action.

The Power of Story on the Brain

In 2010, a group of researchers at Princeton University wanted to explore how communication between a speaker and listener affected the brain. They sat participants down in pairs and instructed the speaker to tell the listener a personal, unrehearsed story. Using sensitive imaging equipment, they scanned each participant's brains during the communication.

For example, one participant (the speaker) shared a story with another participant (the listener) about attending her high school prom. As the speaker told the story, researchers could see how the story affected the brains of both the speaker and listener.

What they discovered was that both the speaker's and the listener's brains engaged in what they called "neural coupling."[2] As the listener heard the story for the first time, his brain activated the same areas as the speaker who was telling the story. This was a remarkable discovery that suggests that stories act as "mental stimulation." In other words, when we hear a story, the same regions of the brain that would be stimulated if we had experienced the circumstances of the story ourselves are activated.[3] In a sense, the act of neural coupling is an act of empathy.

---

2 [Stephens]

3 [Oatley]

It's our brain's way of placing us in the circumstances of the storyteller and allowing us to feel and experience the same moments.

This is why storytelling has stood the test of time and why oral traditions still exist. If you've ever experienced a profound life event, like a near-death experience, you can probably remember the countless times you were asked to recount the story for your friends and family. Everyone wants to hear what happened, and while you take them through the details, they're asking themselves, "I wonder what I would've done in that situation?" Essentially, our brains are allowing us to learn from one another's experience. When we hear the story of a friend whose car was totaled in a collision at a nearby intersection, our brains make a note to move through that intersection more carefully in the future. Conversely, if our friend has lost weight while trying a new diet and exercise routine, we want to hear the story so that we can achieve similar results. Stories are the vehicle by which we share our profound successes and our humbling mistakes.

Modern science and centuries of historical evidence indicate that if you want to inspire others to learn and grow, you must become a great storyteller. Stories are the vehicle by which you will drive change and inspire others to adopt the three vital behaviors: awareness, curiosity, and courage.

Companies with great cultures understand this. They invest in professional resources to craft stories, videos, internal intranet blogs, posters, and other media. They know that to inspire or even maintain a movement, their organizations need to be inspired by compelling stories of excellence.

Inspiring Others to Action

As we began to hit our stride in DevDiv, we saw that customer interviews, surveys, concept-value tests, and usability testing were on the rise. It was fantastic to see the energy our product teams were bringing to these interactions and the insights they were gaining from connecting with our customers.

Our team experimented with running "Customer-Driven Alumni" events to try to build community among employees who had gone through our workshops. Although that's been something that's been difficult to grow organically, I still delight in the first two groups we were able to gather. In fact, a conversation I had with the second group still stands out to me.

When I asked the group, "So, what's the biggest problem you've been having with this customer-driven way of building software? Anyone have anything they've been frustrated with?"

I expected to hear the common frustrations I had already heard from our various product teams. What I expected to hear was about how challenging it was to find customers. I expected to hear how difficult it was to find time in the day to talk to customers. These were the common complaints from the early days.

However, one program manager mentioned a frustration that we hadn't heard before.

She said, "You know, it's actually going pretty well. I've gotten some really good data and I've really enjoyed talking to our customers and learning how they use our products."

Then, addressing the group, she asked, "I'm wondering how any of you handle handoffs. I have some really good notes and data on these customer calls I've been having. I'm going to be moving onto another project, and I just feel like everything I experienced is going to be lost when I hand it over to someone else."

In more private settings, we heard that product team members enjoyed the connections they were making with their customers but were frustrated by how much data it took to move a decision forward.

To me, the connection between those two frustrations is woven into a single thread. It's not easy to tell a story with just data alone.

The program manager who worried about handing over her project was struggling because she had real empathy for the customers she had met. She was afraid that the stories of those customers couldn't be captured in spreadsheets and raw interview notes. If she handed the project to someone else, the momentum of the project she had worked on so hard would be lost.

In the more private conversations, those team members were frustrated by inaction. The feeling was that they'd "done all the right things" and had been "data driven," but their data wasn't enough to drive action within the rest of the division. In effect, were being "data rich and action poor."

Essentially, both of those situations occur because, fundamentally, the story gets lost. The nuance. The essence of the customer. It's difficult to scale customer empathy because empathy is experienced. It's difficult to transfer empathy through emails or project status updates. A customer complaint given in a bug/fix report can be hard to empathize with and even harder to be motivated by. "Data can persuade people, but it doesn't inspire them to act," says bestselling author and executive coach Harrison Monarth.[4]

So, how do you scale that kind of customer empathy from team to team? Well, consider the way we humans have been exchanging data for centuries. We've told one another stories. Stories give us the meaningful information in a way that sticks. Stories are easy to share and, if done the right way, can drive emotion in us. A great story can make us laugh, cry, or change the way we see the world.

Consider the story you're reading now. How convincing would it have been if I had given it to you in an Excel spreadsheet? If this story was given to you as a set of raw notes, would you have been able to easily ascertain the fundamental learnings of our transformation? Probably not.

---

4 [Zak-Paul]

Yet, recalling a meaningful story is effortless for us. That's why hearing stories of our customers can be so meaningful; these stories can drive us into action.

THE IMPACT LADDER

Let's consider the following analogy. Imagine that I went on an African safari. During my visit, I had a transformative experience, seeing a herd of elephants move across the savanna. Directly witnessing the majesty of these elephants, the way they care for one another and raise their young, I now realize how important it is to protect these animals.

Our safari guide tells us that these elephants are listed on the endangered species list and that, in Africa, their populations have seen the worst decline in the past 25 years. I'm distraught to learn that this herd was attacked by poachers only months earlier. Hunters had killed nearly half of them, stealing their ivory for the black market.

Seeing their beauty and fragility firsthand, I understand the urgency and the importance of conservation.

Then, I travel back home to Seattle.

I feel compelled to share the transformative experience I had with family, friends, and colleagues. I want them to truly appreciate how important it is that we take care of these animals. Perhaps I start a campaign and try to raise money to donate to the African Wildlife Foundation. I'm inspired and I want to do my part.

In Seattle, far away from the savanna, many of my peers fail to grasp the sense of urgency that I have. They have never been to Africa. Sure, they've seen an elephant at the zoo, and some of them might have even heard they were endangered, but there are so many other urgent, closer-to-home issues that they are concerned with. I retweet the latest news and reports on Twitter and share heartbreaking articles about hunted elephants on Facebook. Out of all my friends and colleagues, I get one response back: a sad-face emoji.

Slowly my frustration mounts. "Why can't people see how important this is?!"

When we consider the level of impact I have in this situation, we can look at my level of influence along an *Impact Ladder* (see Figure 7-1). Essentially, we can move through the stages of empathy others will have with my story of the elephants.

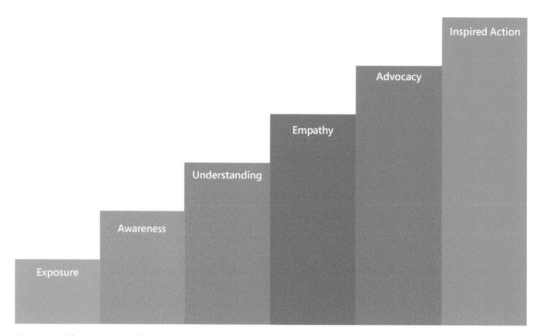

Figure 7-1. The Impact Ladder

The first stage is exposure: being exposed to the fact that there are endangered elephants in Africa. Then, my friends become aware of the problem of poaching and illegal hunting. I try to move them to understanding why the problem occurs and then build empathy for the pain, suffering, and loss being endured by these animals and why the problem is so important.

But that's not enough. Empathy isn't enough when trying to convince others to do something as a result of newfound information. You need to move people from empathy to advocacy. They join you on your mission to get the word out and bring awareness to the issue, and finally, the ultimate goal is to move them to inspired action. Inspired action is when you've convinced a group of people that the situation with the elephants is so dire, they *must act now*.

So, how do you move people from just being exposed to the issue of endangered elephants, to being completely inspired into action?

The very best way would be to take my family, friends, and colleagues on another safari with me. As they sit in the same spot where I sat, looking down on a sunset-drenched savanna and listening to the safari guide explain the nuances of the herd of elephants in the field, there's a good chance they'd say, "OK. I get it now. I need to do my part to protect these elephants." There's really no better way to convince someone of a problem or opportunity than to create a way for them to experience it for themselves.

We know that creating a coexperienced model of learning is incredibly effective, but it's not always feasible to take every potential donor to the savanna to convince them that saving the elephants is worthwhile. Although we should always strive for creating firsthand experience, it isn't always achievable. For a customer-driven culture, we should emphasize, as much as possible, firsthand experiences with customers. For situations in which that's not possible, we need to get creative. As discussed in Chapter 4, this is what Scott Guthrie did when he had his senior leadership team try to use Azure. He manufactured a firsthand experience for his team to truly feel how difficult it was to get started using the service.

If we refer to the Impact Ladder, we can consider the various levels of empathy I might generate from the strategies I employ. Let's look at each stage of the ladder and how it relates to my ability to relay the elephants' situation:

Exposure

When my coworkers ask about my trip, I mention how awful it is that elephants are still being hunted illegally.

Awareness

During a team meeting, I tell my coworkers about the experience I had and remind them how important it is to care for wildlife.

Understanding

I send around an article I found online that talks about the issues of illegal hunting in Africa and its effects on the elephant population. It includes the most recent population numbers, showing an alarming decline.

Empathy

I create a PowerPoint presentation with pictures from my trip. In my presentation, I talk about my personal transformation, what I've learned about elephants, and why it's so important to protect them.

Advocacy

I create a "Save the Elephants of the Savanna" social network group where people can gather and share the latest updates, articles, and plan meetups and rallies.

Inspired Action

I create an online documentary video series that follows a herd of elephants on a harrowing journey across the savanna. Each elephant is given a name and viewers delight in each animal's unique personality. I design clothing items that are emblazoned with each elephant and their names. The merchandise develops a fan base as people begin to identify with Abioye (the leader of the herd), Sabella (the wise mother), and Rab (the mischievous youngster). The documentary and clothing become a sensation, the proceeds go to protecting the elephants, and the public begins to appreciate just how precious these animals are.

Moving away from the elephants as an example, we can see the parallels of how this same experience can be true when sharing our learnings from customers with other product makers.

I can go on a site visit and spend time with a customer in Charleston, but I'd have the same difficulties convincing my team of the problems and frustrations with the product that I saw when I return to Seattle.

I could share a spreadsheet that has the number of times "Customer A" encountered an issue with the product, but that's unlikely to move the team beyond awareness and understanding. To move toward inspired action and a sense of empathy with the problem, I can push to get teammates to go on at least one site visit with me or show videos of customers experiencing the issue and have them express how frustrating it is when they encounter it. Hearing about the problem in the customer's own words can create a vivid story that inspires the team into action.

How Stories Affect Our Brains

A study conducted at Claremont Graduate University found that the brain releases powerful hormones when we watch videos of character-driven stories or in-person testimonials. In the study, researchers played a video for participants that showed an interview of a father talking about how his son was dying from a brain tumor. Blood was drawn before and after watching the video, and it was determined that there was an increase in oxytocin in the participants who had been exposed to the heart-wrenching interview. Oxytocin is produced in the hypothalamus and is responsible for social bonding, empathy, and generosity.

In fact, along with taking samples of the study participants' blood, researchers also tracked how much money was donated to the foundation featured in the video. For the group that had watched the video, not only did their levels of oxytocin rise, but they also donated more money to the foundation compared to the groups that had not watched the video. Even more, the researchers could accurately predict the amount of money that would be donated, based on the levels of oxytocin that was in the participant's body.[5]

Effectively, great stories have a profound effect on our brain's chemistry, and they have the power to inspire us to action. As we begin to appreciate this, a simple question remains: what makes a great story?

The Patterns of a Great Story

In their book *Made to Stick: Why Some Ideas Survive and Others Die*, Chip and Dan Heath deconstruct the most effective stories. In their research, they've identified that all great stories contain five patterns, each of which we explore in the subsections that follow.

---

5 [Mosendz]

SIMPLICITY

Great storytellers break messages down to their essentials. They're selective and only hold on to the parts of the story that matter. It's surprisingly difficult to tell a simple story when conveying a complex idea, but it's important not to overload your messages with too many ideas. If your message is complicated and multifaceted, you end up trying to communicate everything, and in the end, you communicate nothing. To have an effective message, break down complex ideas into singular, memorable ideas. Simple words and phrases to sum up larger more complex points make your stories sticky and memorable.

UNEXPECTEDNESS

Great stories break the script. They bring new information to light in unexpected ways. Our brains are computers that thrive on collecting new and novel information, filtering out data that we've seen before. Today, our brains are being pummeled with more information than ever before. Emails, television ads, and app notifications produce an incredible amount of noise in the signal, and it can be very difficult for us to determine what information is worth paying attention to.

In a 2014 memo released to the public, Satya said, "We are moving from a world where computing power was scarce to a place where it now is almost limitless, and where the true scarce commodity is increasingly human attention."[6] We must find ways to cut through the noise and capture people's attention. Breaking the script and offering data in new ways can be a great way to do that.

For example, a talented design manager named Jaclyn Shumate from our Office Media Group came up with a novel solution to share customer learnings with her team. Because her team was responsible for Stream, an enterprise-level video-sharing service, she decided to use the service to produce a video series much like a nightly news segment. With music, sound effects, direct clips from customer interviews, and a bit of humor, she created a fun and engaging way for her team to hear the latest round of customer feedback. By making sharing fun, she was able to capture the entire team's attention and get them excited about learning directly from the customer.

CONCRETENESS

Mission statements and messages that are intended to inspire change can often go awry if they feel ambiguous or abstract. Saying things like "empathize with your customers" or "create delightful experiences" can prove problematic when put into action. Our brains need concrete examples or tightly aligned analogies to break down complex messages into meaning that we can act upon.

---

6 [Geary]

CREDIBILITY

Any message or story must be backed with authenticity. Authentic stories help listeners trust the message. If your message or story feels like a platitude or an empty promise, discerning listeners will sense that. The best change agents are those who find ways to remain passionate about their mission. To maintain credibility, they're always learning and looking for new ideas to help shape their company's culture.

EMOTIONS

Studies show that we remember the stories that move us. When a story gets us to feel something, whether it be inspiration or disgust, it has the power to get us to confront our own beliefs and behaviors. In business settings, we often shy away from talking about emotions. Particularly in North America, we've been conditioned to believe that "business isn't personal." However, if you want an organization that is deeply committed to delivering the best for your customers, you need to get comfortable with sharing your customers' emotions. If customers are frustrated, don't sterilize those comments. If a customer is cursing with frustration or slamming their fists on the table, make sure all the product teams see it. These emotions make the work we do real and are a potent reminder of the impact, negative or positive, that we all have on our customers.

Using Metaphors to Make Your Ideas Accessible

One difficult thing about working in DevDiv is that the situations we encounter with customers can be very difficult to communicate to people who are uninitiated with the technology.

For example, we were working with a team that was exploring opportunities for customers using Node.js, a runtime environment that allows developers to build applications. One of the things that makes Node.js unique is that it uses JavaScript, an incredibly popular programming language used by millions of developers. In a way, Node.js legitimized JavaScript as a language that could be used in highly scalable applications, proving that JavaScript was for more than just website development.

After talking with various Node.js customers, the team discovered that there were two primary customer segments. Both were still learning Node.js, but one segment already knew how to write code in JavaScript, and the other segment did not.

As we analyzed and synthesized the data from our interviews, the team went back-and-forth trying to articulate the similarities and differences between these two groups, which were numerous.

Finally, one of the program managers on the team said, "You know, it's sort of like swimming. Developers who already know how to write JavaScript are like swimmers who are good at swimming in the pool. The developers who don't know JavaScript can't swim at all. Taking both types of developers and getting them to use Node.js is like throwing the pool swimmer and the nonswimmer in the ocean. The developers who know JavaScript can tread water, but now they're encountering all sorts of new challenges, like a pool swimmer would encounter trying to navigate the massive waves and choppy water. The developers who don't know Java-Script are like people trying to learn to swim for the first time, in the ocean! It's hopeless!"

These types of metaphors, when accompanied by real customer stories, act as "shortcuts" and can help us empathize with another person's experience. Expert storytellers help broader audiences understand complex ideas by relating the concept to an experience they're more familiar with.

In his book *I Is an Other: The Secret Life of Metaphor and How It Shapes the Way We See the World*, author James Geary explains how metaphors and analogies help us generate empathy and understanding:

> *Analogy is the only way we learn about anything of which we can have no direct experience, whether it's the behavior of subatomic particles or the content of other people's experiences.[7]*

Through our past experiences of learning how to swim, we could empathize with how it must feel to learn Node.js. It helped us appreciate just how difficult it would be for each customer segment to learn Node.js. Each segment had its own frustrations, but the amount of JavaScript they already knew helped us determine the intensity of those frustrations.

The customers we talk to offer us their real stories and unique perspectives. We can then take the responses of each customer and put them on a customer card (see Figure 7-2). A collection of these cards can represent an entire customer segment. In a culture that employs the power of customer voices, you don't need to spend time designing a fictitious persona. Your team will be armed with customer profiles full of real customers the team has talked to.

---

7 [Geary]

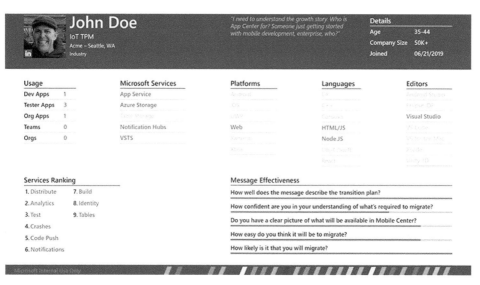

Figure 7-2. An example of a customer card, combining data from product usage, survey responses, and direct interviews

Don't Just Tell Them, Show Them

Like spoken metaphors, visual metaphors can also be a powerful way to communicate complex ideas. The adage "a picture is worth a thousand words" holds true, and every great storyteller thinks not only in words, but in pictures as well.

Although numerical data and statistics can bring credibility and authority, they also increase the chances that our overall message will become buried by calculations and normalizations. If we're not careful, numbers can pull the human condition out of the stories that we want share. To get to the essence of any story, you need the "five Ws": the who, what, where, when, and why.

Dan Roam, author of *Blah, Blah, Blah: What to Do When Words Don't Work*, advocates using simple illustrations to communicate big ideas. Things like graphs, stick figure characters, smiley and sad faces, and sketches of everyday objects help us connect the storyteller's message to concepts we're already familiar with.

Roam promotes the use of a "vivid grammar," which aligns the words in our stories to visual aids that can help make them more vivid.[8]

We were inspired by this and developed our own "vivid grammar" graph to be used in our workshops.

---

8 [Roam]

Table 7-1 shows how our version of Roam's vivid grammar graph breaks down.

Table 7-1. Vivid grammar graph

Grammar	Visual
Who/what Person, place, thing, context	 Portrait
How much Some, few, enough, most, less, all	 Charts
Where Above, below, and, or, but	 Maps

Grammar	Visual
When Before, now, later	 Timelines
How Simple relationships	 Flowcharts
Why Complex relationships	 Multivariable plots
Moral Key takeaway	$$E = mc^2$$ Equations

Within this table, we identify the grammar, which is the type of story we're trying to tell, and the corresponding visual element that helps us visualize that type of story. This has proven to be an invaluable tool when our product teams need to express what they've learned from their customers.

Let's examine each grammar in detail:

Who/what (nouns and pronouns)

As we discussed earlier, a customer's quotes, pictures, and other vivid information can be used to create a customer card. A collection of those cards could represent an entire customer profile. When customers participate in our research studies or give us feedback, we can ask for their permission to use additional resources like their LinkedIn profiles. Often, customers are more than willing to share this information given that it is available to the public anyway. These profiles can provide rich information that bring the customer to life for the rest of the team.

How much (adjectives of quantity)

When you're dealing with quantity, it can be useful to take the time to plot the differences on a bar graph or pie chart. For instance, it can be useful to see how much money customers are spending to resolve a problem or how much time is required to learn a new tool. When these quantities are displayed visually, they can be powerful visuals that help teams understand the magnitude of their customers' issues.

Where (prepositions and conjunctions)

When trying to communicate position, location, or how different ideas relate to one another, a map can be a valuable instrument to show those representations. Tension graphs that show how two needs are at odds with another (e.g., cost versus quality) can help teams appreciate the conflicts our customers face when making decisions to choose our products.

When (tense)

As you spend time learning from customers, it might become necessary to capture when an important event occurs. Timelines can help us chart our culture change journey or how a customer uses our products. For example, the team might benefit from seeing your customer's experience plotted over a *journey timeline*. The timeline could show critical moments when the customer needs to interact with your product. A tool like a journey timeline can help illustrate the points in time when the customer experience of your product can be improved.

How? (complex verbs)

When you're trying to illustrate what happened or how something occurs, flowcharts can be useful tools to visualize those procedural operations. Our customers can often live and work within complex worlds and relationships. For example, if your team works on collaboration software, it can be useful for it to visualize and understand how customers navigate their leadership chain to seek approval for project funding. The subtle nuances in how these customers collaborate within these contexts can surface valuable unmet needs for a team focused on organizational collaboration.

Why? (complex subjects)

If you're trying to communicate why something is happening in your data, illustrations like multivariable plots can help visualize how different factors relate to one another and produce a particular outcome. For example, you might use a multivariable plot to show how variables like time, money, or prior investment affect a customer's decision to try your product. Plotting these variables together can illuminate the strength, form, and dependence they have on one another.

Moral

Every story should have a moral or theme. It's the "big idea" or shortcut that sums it all up. Earlier, we looked at the story of a team working with Node.js customers. They came up with the metaphor of pool swimmers and nonswimmers being thrust into learning how to swim in the ocean. The moral to the insight of that story could be as simple as, "Node.js is like learning to swim in the ocean." These morals act as a sort of equation, helping you to create shortcuts to understanding by creating metaphors to more familiar experiences. Morals act as a tagline: an idea you can convey quickly, without having to unpack everything.

Consider the customer stories that are shared in your organization. Are they filled with numbers and statistics, or do you include in-depth customer stories and illustrations that help teams to understand your learnings? Are you finding ways to combine the power of quantitative data (numbers) with the emotion of qualitative data (direct customer observations, quotes, testimonials)?

In turn, consider your culture change movement. Are your stories of success consumed with training completion scores or pledge signups? Do you have rich, vivid testimonials from fellow employees that share their experiences with the new culture change? What are the morals of these stories, and what should your fellow employees learn from them?

CONSIDER THE MEDIUM

Sometimes, it can be a slog to look at bland notes on a PowerPoint slide or read through a dense trip report. If you want teams to empathize with customers, consider delivering the information in novel ways. The "culture room" that we built for Satya's visit (see Chapter 1) is an example of this.

Every time we bring someone new into the room, we delight in their reaction. We hear things such as, "I like how I feel in this room; it feels like I'm surrounded by great ideas." Or, we hear, "Did you do something with the lighting in the room? I feel so alert and creative!" Now, even though we're proud of the learnings shared in the room, I can confidently state that we had nothing to do with the lighting in the room.

What I think is happening during those visits is that people in business have become so used to receiving data in certain forms that it's rare when they see something that breaks the script. Giving someone a presentation that takes over a physical room isn't what they're expecting. They're expecting to sit in a darkened conference room, pleading with their eyes not to close.

So, if you're having trouble sparking desired action for your latest initiative, you might need to consider how you're delivering the learnings that support your project. Think of delivering your learning in ways that might break the mold of expectation. For example, we have had teams create "customer walls" with quotes from customer interviews or pictures customers have given us permission to use. They'll be strategically placed in hallways so that team members can catch a customer story on the way to their next meeting. I always delight when I see a product team surrounding one of these installations, reflecting on our products and discussing ways to better serve our customers. Consider how you can feature your customer feedback in unexpected ways for your product teams. In effect, you want to *surround* them with their customers so that they see the impact they're making as they go about their work. With your customers' permission, you can take their feedback and showcase it by hanging posters in your hallways or pushing it out to screensavers or televisions in your building. This can create a visual experience throughout your offices that keep your teams connected to the customers they serve.

Vivid Stories Are Directly Proportional to Vivid Interviews

Our ability to tell vivid stories is directly proportional to our ability to conduct vivid interviews with our customers. In other words, if we're not asking vivid questions, we cannot tell vivid stories. If we limit our interviews to closed yes-or-no questions, we will be left with a bunch of data but no stories to share.

For example, suppose that I'm doing an investigation into how people respond to a new dashboard we're designing in a car. I could take a group of customers who have been using the revised dashboard and ask them simply:

Do you like the new dashboard?

We could imagine a variety of simple responses. Customers might say things like, "Sure. It's good," or, "No. It's confusing."

I could close our study and report on the number of customers who liked the new dashboard versus the number of customers who didn't like it. Of course, the next logical question the team might have is, "Why did they like or dislike it?"

By asking open-ended questions, we can help customers give us much more vivid information about their experiences. We can ask questions like these:

What has your experience been like using the dashboard?

When was the last time you configured a setting on your dashboard? What was the experience like?

How often would you say that you use the dashboard?

What components of the dashboard are most important? What components are the least important?

What motivated you to configure the dashboard?

Would you recommend the new dashboard to a friend? Why or why not?

If you were able to change one thing about the dashboard, what would it be?

These questions allow the customers to tell us a story that highlights their personal motivations, their frustrations, and their desires. As customers respond, we continually ask them to tell us more.

Open-ended, vivid questions help our customers reflect on their experiences, think deeply about how our products affect them, and give them permission to challenge us and tell us how we can improve the experience for them.

The answers they give us to these questions give us the anecdotes that we need to bring their stories and experiences to life.

Steve Portigal, author and user research consultant, says that your goal is to move your interviews from "Question-Answer" to "Question-Story." He suggests that, by continuing to ask follow-up questions and digging deeper into your customer responses, you will help customers share their personal experiences.[9] You're also building a rapport and a relationship with the customer, getting to know who they really are.

In just about any engineering review, you'll hear Julia Liuson, John Montgomery, or Amanda Silver ask questions like: "What customers did you talk to?" "What did you ask them?" "What did they have to say?" Our leadership team is trying to grasp the bigger picture. They're asking for the story. Teams have learned quickly that they need to be armed with these stories in order to communicate how a change in a product or service will affect our customers.

As you've seen throughout this book, the same can be said of the stories you share around your culture change. Asking employees rich, vivid, open-ended questions is a great way to get to the heart of their stories of change. These are the details that inspire others to enact the three vital behaviors of change (awareness, curiosity, and courage). Seeing stories of employees succeeding with the new cultural values can motivate others to engage and participate.

---

9 [Tate-Portigal]

Author and cognitive neuroscientist Tali Sharot says that "People observe not only your choices but also the consequences you experience as a result of those choices. This is why behavior has widespread consequences—it affects not only the person being praised or critiqued but also everyone else who is watching."[10]

Applying the Hack

Here are some ways that you can make your data more relatable:

- It's important that your teams' vivid customer stories become part of everyday conversation. Resist the urge to hold onto customer feedback in favor of an extensive report.

- Consider taking a creative writing course or studying the key elements of storytelling. Practicing these skills can have a huge impact in communicating culture change. Study other great storytellers in your organization or industry. When you see their stories, what captivates you? How do they get your attention?

- Look over the ways that you share customer information. Are your customers just nameless numbers and statistics? If so, make time to feature the faces and voices of real customers. You can do this through video, presentation, inviting them to visit the team, and many other methods. The point is to connect the team with the real people they serve.

- As you and your teams collect customer stories, look over them and consider how they can best be used to inspire others. Often, you'll find ways to use a great story in multiple venues (e.g., staff meetings, division-wide newsletters, product presentations, etc.).

- Dedicate a wall in your team room as the "Customer Wall." This can be a space where the team hangs pictures, quotes, interview notes, or any other learning about the customer. It can be a creative way for everyone to participate in customer learning.

- Focus on telling the *complete* story. Don't just focus on sharing how your customer is using the product. Share with them *who* the customer is. Don't forget to include vital learnings like what motivates them, what frustrates them, or what they value. A customer isn't just a user of your product; they're a human being with emotions and a story. Be sure that your teams capture those vivid elements.

- How visual is the story you're trying to tell? Are you relying only on text and numbers? Pictures, graphs, and flowcharts go a long way in simplifying complex stories.

---

10 [Sharot]

- Write a summary paragraph of your learnings from customer interviews. Then, condense those findings into two sentences. Then, a single sentence. Finally, a single word. Try expressing your big ideas in multiple ways, long form and short.

- Always consider your audience. Each time you tell the story of your customers, there will be something meaningful for each group you meet with. Before each meeting, review your work and ask yourself, "What will this team or person care most about?" and devise a way to get those things as soon as possible.

- Try "breaking the script" by delivering your findings in novel and unexpected ways. Instead of an emailed report, perhaps you can design a wall just outside your leadership team's office. Make it visual and colorful. Experiment with scale and space. Record a "breaking news" video in the format of late-night news, flashing on the latest customer interviews. Break people out of their day-to-day expectations to gain their attention and interest.

- If you're dealing with a complex idea, consider aligning your points to a concept that is more accessible and familiar. Imagine that you're explaining your work to your grandparents. What analogies would you use to help them understand what you've learned?

- Bring energy to your storytelling! Your audience will feed off the energy you give. If you're passionate and excited about what you've learned, let that show through.

- Don't be tempted to paraphrase or summarize customer reactions. Saying things like, "Customers really hated this," or, "Nobody noticed it," creates too much distance between the team and the customers' emotions. For example, sharing a quote from a customer that says, "You know, I really loved this product until you introduced this new change. Now, I'll never use it again. You've lost me as a customer," is far more powerful than simply saying "customers really don't like the new feature."

Measuring Change

In *The Physiology of Taste*, author Jean Anthelme wrote, "Tell me what you eat and I will tell you what you are." More than a century later, this statement has taken a much broader meaning to suggest that "you are what you eat."

What we measure has the same effect on our organizations as the food we put in our bodies. The metrics we use to enforce accountability is where our cultural platitudes are tested. How we define and measure success is the final test that reveals what we truly value as an organization. Dov Seidman, author and business philosopher, says, "What we choose to measure is a window into our values, and into *what* we value. Because if you measure something, you're telling people that it matters."[1]

In the opening chapter of this book, we talked about how we "Hacked our Culture" in Dev-Div. Essentially, we moved the organization forward by instituting a new language that encouraged new behaviors and thinking, which ultimately changed our values and our culture.

But how do you *measure* an effect like this? How are you able to quantify your progress and prove that your change efforts are working? It's not as simple as tracking something like Net Promoter Score (NPS) or customer satisfaction. Of course, measures like these are important in a customer-driven organization, because customer satisfaction is paramount. However, these numbers are less reliable in determining employee satisfaction.

It could be said that your metrics are just as powerful as any leader in your organization. Your metrics are the currency of your organization. It's the measuring stick that every team compares themselves to. Metrics define what impact looks like for your organization.

However, not all measures for cultural growth can be neatly categorized on a daily dashboard. You'll need a holistic approach that utilizes both quantitative and qualitative feedback. When measuring change, you'll need to exhibit the three vital behaviors:

---

1 [Doerr] p. 220

Awareness

    Realize that cultural health can't be defined by revenue or customer satisfaction scores alone.

Curiosity

    Maintain a constant desire to learn from your employees and customers and define how cultural change is manifesting itself in product growth.

Courage

    Be willing to admit when a business metric is at odds with a customer-driven metric and have the courage to adjust your approach.

In this chapter, we explore how to think about measuring cultural change, and we look at some of the things that DevDiv has measured to track our own cultural progress.

Unfortunately, there isn't a one-size-fits-all strategy. However, we can still reflect on the six cultural hacks and see how they show up in the way DevDiv measures its progress.

"Multiplier Metrics" Versus "Diminisher Metrics"

When discussing the metrics that you should be using to measure your change effort, it's good to go back to when we discussed Liz Wiseman's work in her book *Multipliers: How Leaders Make Everyone Smarter* (see "Be a Multiplier" on page 65).

We talked about how *multipliers* are leaders who can unlock their teams' true passions and genius. Conversely, *diminishers* are those who seek to penalize or control genius, leaving teams frustrated or disconnected from their overall purpose. Wiseman also suggests that leaders can also be "accidental diminishers," unaware that they are negatively affecting their employees.

The same can be true of metrics. Your metrics are the ultimate belonging cue. For example, if you want a culture that embraces a language of learning, you can't be overreliant on metrics that prove only when you're right.

Does that mean you have to run an organization that is ambivalent about revenue going down or costs going up? Of course not. However, we must evaluate how we plan to measure culture change and ensure we're not diminishing or contradicting our mission.

Consider this example: imagine that we are kicking off our customer-driven culture-change initiative. As part of the change effort, our team has a series of interactive workshops that we plan to give all employees. We have a sizeable organization, so it's going to take time to get employees the new tools they need to operate in the new culture.

After a few months, the director of the organization sees the attendance reports of the workshops and is dismayed because she sees that not all of them have been at capacity. This is incredibly frustrating, because these workshops cost money and resources that she fought hard for. She's already committed to her leadership team that all employees would be trained by the end of the fiscal year. At this rate, she'll be lucky to secure a third of the employees she's committed.

This might cause her to have one of two reactions:

Diminisher

The director decides to create a list of everyone who has *not* attended the training. She sends an organization-wide email thanking all the employees who have attended the training thus far. The remaining employees are "strongly encouraged" to complete the training as soon as possible.

To her management team, she sends an email with lists of "tardy" employees. The implication is that the managers should make it their priority to bring these employees in line.

The managers begin writing emails to their team members, pushing hard for complete attendance.

Multiplier

The director is aware that this is only one signal. It is indeed alarming, but there are so many factors that could be contributing to why attendance isn't where it should be.

She decides to put a small team together and come up with some hypotheses as to why attendance is low. They divide and conquer, talking to as many employees as they can over the next few days. They ask questions of the employees who attended the workshop and those who have not. They're curious to understand what they can do to make it easier for employees to attend and get the most meaning out of it. She knows that this high-touch, intimate feedback is a crucial metric to the complete picture.

After talking with employees, they begin to identify some common themes. First, the employees are clearly overwhelmed by the different workshops the team is offering. They're confused about which training they need and need better ways to see what time workshops are available.

That was a disappointing finding, but the team has an idea to put a schedule up on the company intranet site, giving employees more visibility into when the trainings are available.

Finally, the director has the courage to go back to her leadership and update them on the disappointing attendance results. However, she comes to the meeting with promising news, too. After talking with employees, it's clear that the workshops are being positively received. Employees who have attended are giving very positive feedback. There's a desire to attend the workshops and join the new culture; it's just proving difficult logistically.

She proposes a new strategy to her leaders. They'll continue monitoring attendance, but they'll continue to collect feedback on the ground and determine how the workshops can be improved. She also has a plan to share employee testimonials to give others an authentic look at the excitement being built up on the ground. She has low-cost ways to distribute these stories through existing channels, so she's not asking for more money; she just needs more time to see whether these adjustments will affect attendance.

Both strategies have merit and might even produce the exact outcome (e.g., more employees in attendance). However, the multiplier approach encapsulates the bigger picture. It embraces the three vital behaviors of awareness, curiosity, and courage. For the multiplier, attendance scores are a factor, and she's monitoring it carefully, but the director is aware that there could be other factors other than laziness or rebellion. She continues with curiosity to hear from the employees themselves. The director is leading with a learning mindset, investing her resources carefully, and moving in a lean and iterative way. Finally, she has the courage to admit that she made a mistake. She hasn't failed because she's already delivering a revised plan that incorporates her latest learnings.

In this example, the director modeled the three vital behaviors (awareness, curiosity, and courage) to her entire management staff. Inspired by her approach, her staff decided to engage their employees as well, asking for feedback on how they can make it easier for them to attend the workshops.

Employees give critical but supportive feedback on how things can be improved. They're invested in the culture change because they want to see positive change as well. Having this dialogue with their managers helps them feel a part of the conversation. They're empowered to get involved and help shape the new culture. That positive goodwill encourages even the most stubborn employee to reconsider their position.

Additionally, because the director had the courage to admit a mistake, there's not a lot of drama around the event. Managers aren't distracted from the overall mission and they quickly pivot their approach. As they have conversations with their employees, they're actively sharing their learnings with one another.

Objectives and Key Results

In the book *Measure What Matters*, author John Doerr outlines a new approach to measuring progress, pioneered by Intel founder and former CEO Andy Grove. It's a system that relies on Objectives and Key Results (OKRs), and it's a way to clearly define what you want to achieve, why you want to achieve it, and how you will know whether you've met the objective. According to Doerr, Grove believed that culture was a manual for making quicker and more reliable decisions.[2]

---

2 [Doerr] p. 213

Objectives function as your overarching goal, whereas key results are the measurements you employ to determine whether you are contributing to that goal. OKRs are intended to be lightweight and iterative but provide enough direction and accountability to track progress.

For an example, let's look at Caesar's Entertainment. The company is a casino gaming and hospitality giant and owner of the world-famous Caesar's Palace casino resort in Las Vegas, Nevada. The resort is located on "The Strip," which nestles it between many other renowned hotels like The Bellagio, The MGM Grand, and the Venetian. With this kind of competition, the choices are infinite for guests to pick a hotel that meets their needs. Additionally, Caesar's Palace is only one of the company's 40 US resorts.

To do this, it must multiply and motivate nearly 75,000 people, to get them to align their day-to-day job with exceptional customer service. That's one of many objectives for the company.

Vice President of Total Service Terry Byrnes says they achieved this by creating a system that ties employee incentives to the quality service employees provide their customers. That's why his team developed an incentive program that rewards employees for going above and beyond for their customers.

Byrne's team analyzes guest survey data to find correlations between customer ratings and brand loyalty. It identified key thresholds that would indicate return business. Essentially, when customers gave a certain target of good reviews, they would often become return visitors.

When resorts exceed these thresholds, their employees are awarded points that can be used to buy real-world merchandise from a sponsored website.

The key result could be how many bankable points have been awarded to each result. This would be a great indicator to determine whether employees are engaging in customer obsession. Additionally, if resorts are receiving too many points, maybe it's time to revisit the thresholds and raise the standard of excellence; what a great problem to have!

The points provided by Caesar's Entertainment to its employees are a multiplier metric. They've aligned a desired outcome with a desired behavior and measured it in a way that doesn't diminish employees' willingness to participate. In fact, it's quite the opposite. The points are something employees *want* to accrue, and they are willing to engage in the necessary behaviors to earn them. Additionally, the points are an easy metric to track. Managers can see how many points are being distributed and to whom. These metrics can help them recognize employees who are going the extra mile to create great experiences for their customers. It's a healthy competition that's based on delivering exceptional service.

The points system has worked brilliantly for Caesar's Entertainment. In fact, during an industry dip in travel between 2008 and 2015, Caesar's resorts were able to maintain its lead within the industry in terms of customer satisfaction.[3] Even though the industry was hit with

---

3 [Dyer] pp. 100–102

economic hardship, the employees at Caesar's were still committed to providing a great experience for their customers.

Metrics and Customer Feedback

As we discussed in Chapter 7, we are inspired to action when we're given data that is not only representative, but relatable as well.

In the example earlier in this chapter, the multiplier's team used quantitative data (e.g., attendance records) in conjunction with qualitative data (e.g., direct customer interviews) to create a complete picture of the success of the change effort. The team utilized the metric to strategize about what it needed to collect feedback on. Attendance was low, so it engaged directly with employees to determine why. The team valued the metric and the feedback equally, and it gave them a more complete picture to make decisions going forward.

Consider organizations like Habitat for Humanity, whose mission is to provide everyone in the world with a place to live. It's a global nonprofit that organizes local communities from all over the world to build and repair homes for those in need.

It stands to reason that "the number of homes built or repaired" would certainly be a metric that Habitat for Humanity would care about. It's an indicator of the organization's capacity to build homes. However, is it the only indicator for the level of impact they're having on the world?

Of course not.

Building the homes is a means to an end for Habitat for Humanity. It believes that having a place to live is a key factor in communities becoming self-sufficient, contributing members of the world. It's one of the organization's most important objectives. The number of houses built is one of the many key results.

However, for Habitat for Humanity, there's also another higher-level objective: to prove to donors that providing homes is the best way to improve someone's quality of life. The organization relies on the contributions of others; making a good case is part of inspiring others to action.

When we consider that objective, there are myriad new key results Habitat for Humanity could track: mortality rate, gross domestic product (GDP), high school graduation rates, crime rates, and employment rates. The organization could follow these results to determine whether there are correlations between the work they're doing and the improvement in these numbers.

Of course, they could also track donations to determine their success, but they could also follow the amount of time being donated by volunteers to determine if they're growing the social consciousness.

To measure demonstrable, long-lasting change, Habitat for Humanity needs to gather community feedback, not only looking for ways to improve, but also to ensure that its program is delivering on its mission. If you browse Habitat for Humanity's website, you'll find it covered with stories, quotes, and pictures. These stories are more than just marketing material; they're potent evidence that supports the organization's core hypothesis: having a home dramatically increases your quality of life.

GATHERING EMPLOYEE FEEDBACK

Although Habitat for Humanity is using quantitative and qualitative feedback to gauge its impact for cultural change, you should consider how you can take advantage of the same type of feedback from your *employees* to determine the success of your cultural change efforts.

At Microsoft, the company holds an annual MS Poll, which surveys employee responses on a variety of factors, from effectiveness of our leaders, to the belief that the company is living up to our mission and values.

In a sense, the company is asking its employees, "Are our company values part of your everyday lived experience?"

Additionally, managers are trained to go over MS Poll results with their employees. The results provide transparency and encourage a discussion on what's working and what isn't.

Microsoft also has MS Pulse, which is a smaller survey that is sent to randomly selected employees throughout the year. This allows our leadership team to keep an eye on unexpected fluctuations in employee satisfaction.

The combination of these surveys, plus the corresponding conversations that managers have with their employees, is a great example of combining the *what* (quantitative) along with the *why* (qualitative).

THE CULTURAL HEARTBEAT

Combining quantitative and qualitative feedback creates a healthy "cultural heartbeat" (see Figure 8-1). These signals come together to give you a complete picture into how your culture is growing. For example, if you're seeing high attendance in trainings or workshops but are struggling to come up with stories of success on the ground, it might be an indication that your cultural training isn't as effective as it could be. It also could be an indication of the disconnect of how you're measuring success. With too much emphasis on attendance in workshops and trainings, you're missing more nuanced challenges that are preventing employees from engaging in the vital behaviors that you want them to.

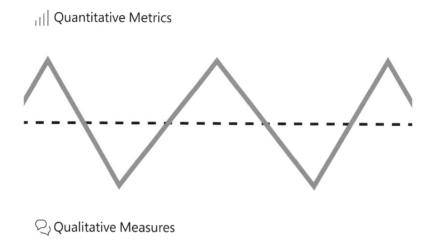

Figure 8-1. Analyzing your organization's "cultural heartbeat" by combining quantitative metrics with qualitative measures

As we began to improve our processes to be more customer driven, we started where many companies do, by looking at our NPS. Fundamentally, NPS centers itself on one question that is asked of customers: would you recommend this product to a friend or colleague? The response to this question is considered an indicator of how satisfied customers are with your product. In a sense, the more they're willing to recommend it to others, the more satisfied they are with the product. NPS has become an industry metric that organizations can use to compare themselves with their competition.

However, improving an NPS can be a terrible motivator for employees. How these scores are calculated can sometimes create a diffusion in understanding. Essentially, NPS can tell you that your customers are dissatisfied, but it can't tell you *why* they're dissatisfied.

"We made a premature causation," John Montgomery says, "that if we fix performance and reliability, Net Promoter Score will rise. It turns out that's not how Net Promoter Score works for us."[4]

Our NPSs didn't improve as a result of us fixing bugs and improving performance. However, we discovered there were other metrics that were improving. "[Looking at our NPSs] opened the door that allowed us to have a conversation about the signal we were getting," John says.

---

4 [Montgomery]

It isn't that we stopped caring about our NPS; it's that we learned that there were other signals we could be looking at to determine our success.

For example, we began monitoring customer sentiment by looking at what customers were saying in interviews, community forums, and social media. We found that, due to our efforts to improve our overall connection with our customers, sentiment toward Microsoft developer tools was improving, and there was a growing positivity toward our offerings. Essentially, as our employees connected with customers, listened to them, and improved the issues they cared most about, our customers shifted from criticizing us to celebrating us.

Measure the Vital Behaviors

Kelly Krout, principal UX research manager in DevDiv, and his team wanted to answer a fundamental question for our organization: was the work we were doing to promote a customer-driven culture inspiring our employees to better connect with customers?

As we discussed in Chapter 2, if you change the language, you change the thinking, which changes the actions and ultimately changes the culture of your entire organization. Armed with this insight, Kelly and his team decided to analyze hundreds of customer notes sent by employees over the same CDNotes email alias we discussed in Chapter 6. This was the email alias where all our employees sent their learnings from customer interviews. Kelly and his team could go as far back as when we began our journey and see how the language of our organization evolved.

What they uncovered astounded us.

First, Kelly's team counted how often our teams were showing curiosity by conducting usability tests, site visits, focus groups, and other customer development methods. The team found that there was a 43% year-over-year growth in these types of activities. They also discovered that the number of customer conversations had grown to a 39% year-over-year growth.

Within the CDNotes emails, the team found a 39% year-over-year growth in the use of terms like "customer" and "user."[5] These terms were now happening just as frequently as "developer," which of course in DevDiv is synonymous with customer because we make developer tools. This finding is encouraging because it suggests that we have grown in our desire to share what we're learning from our customers. Growth in the usage of terms like "customer" and "user" suggested that our division was expanding our definition of the people that use our products. We were seeing them as more than just developers using our tools and services, but as customers and users, too. This was a strong indication that the common language (see Chapter 2) we were building in DevDiv was taking root.

---

5 [Krout]

Kelly and his team also discovered that the quality of our employees' notes on customers were improving over time. By comparing notes that were sent in the early stages of our journey to the notes we were receiving today, we could see that employees were collecting richer and more vivid information about our customers. The types of questions our employees were asking customers improved. The fidelity of their hypotheses improved. The quality of customer feedback improved, and our employees' conversations with customers were generating richer and more vivid insights. Emailed notes from five years ago were sparse and full of online replies to closed questions. Today, we were seeing detailed customer interview reports, full of pictures and direct customer quotes. There were tables that tracked the team's current hypotheses, color-coding them to indicate whether they have been validated, invalidated, or were inconclusive.

Kelly and his team also searched the email alias for terms like "assumption," "hypothesis," and "experiment," as these are key terms that indicate a language of learning.

They discovered a 57% year-over-year growth, sustained over a five-year period, in our employees' use of those terms.

Finally, as we combined the stories of courage we were hearing on the ground—teams experimenting with new ways to learn or pivoting their strategies based on customer feedback —we had strong indicators that our customer-driven culture was growing and that our employees were adopting a learning-first mindset.

Compounded, through mid-2015 to mid-2019 (a four-year period), we saw the following growth:

Change the language (up 141%)
Use of words like "developer," "customer," and "user" to describe our customers

Change the thinking (up 169%)
Use of terms like assumption, hypothesis, validate, invalidate, and experiment

Change the actions—Direct customer observations (up 146%)
Product teams conducting usability tests, focus groups, concept-value tests, and site visits

Change the actions—Direct customer interviews (up 158%)
Product teams talking directly with customers through interviews

As discussed in Chapter 2, Kelly was able to demonstrate that by changing the language, we were able to change our thinking and behaviors within the organization (see Figure 2-1).

Kelly also believes that our business success was a direct result of Satya's call for a customer-obsessed culture.

"His highest goal was customer obsession and creating a great experience for our customers. To think about our customers and learn from our customers." Kelly pauses and starts to chuckle, "And what happens at the same time? We *do* increase revenue and profits. We now have the most valuable company in the world."

"What's in our culture, we're putting it into the products we're building. The customers are getting that back."

Measure Employee Moments

As we've discussed throughout this book, your cultural movement will be defined through the moments you create. Therefore, you should be leaning into those moments when you measure their effectiveness.

There are many defining moments in an employee's career with a company:

- Interviewing for the position
- First day and onboarding
- The beginning and the end of a project
- Performance evaluations and promotions
- Transitioning roles, responsibilities, or teams
- Exiting the company

Each of these moments contains a trove of data that can be used to evaluate your culture.

Like Kelly and his team, what would you find if you were to analyze the language of all your job postings? Would you find language that is consistent with your company's values, especially those regarding being customer driven?

If you were to analyze all the promotions that occurred within your company over the past three years, would you find the reasons listed were consistent with your company's culture? Would these promotions prove that your organization was investing in leaders who were helping build your customer-driven culture?

Employees also have weekly one-on-one discussions with their managers. These are private meetings for each employee to talk with their manager and align work responsibilities. It's also a chance for the employee to discuss anything as it relates to their performance or needs. This ensures that managers are checking in with their employees frequently so they can get ahead of concerns before they become big frustrations.

As you begin to measure the moments that matter to your organization, you should also consider how you can use metrics to create new moments. As Chip and Dan Heath discussed in their book *The Power of Moments*, powerful moments are those that bring elevation, insight, pride, and connection.

For example, each quarter, DevDiv has an "All Hands" meeting. This gathering is one of many opportunities our leadership team uses to address all of the division's employees. In preparation for an event like this, the leadership team will seek out exceptional stories of customer-driven behavior. This action—soliciting managers in the company for great customer-driven stories—is an act of measuring the culture as well. In a sense, if they're having difficulty coming up with great stories to share, that could indicate a problem in the culture worth investigating.

As we've talked about in this book, as a leader or change agent, what you choose to talk about will be a powerful belonging cue to the rest of the organization. If you choose to communicate and focus only on numbers that are in trouble, expect that employees will feel diminished and frustrated. If you continually talk about revenue numbers, your employees will focus on revenue. If you're continually talking about product adoption, your employees will fixate on product adoption.

Like water or electricity, employees' motivations will flow through the paths of least resistance, looking for the best way to drive their own personal growth and impact within the organization. If you only communicate the numbers, the mission will be to improve the numbers.

Margaret J. Wheatley and Myron Kellner-Rodgers, authors and educators in the world of organizational behavior and management, say that managers have become overreliant on numbers to share progress. They believe that gathering and sharing feedback is a vital component in demonstrating growth in any organization. They write:

> *All life thrives on feedback and dies without it. We have to know what is going on around us, how our actions impact others, how the environment is changing, how we're changing. If we don't have access to this kind of information, we can't adapt or grow. Without feedback, we shrivel into routines and develop hard shells that keep newness out. We don't survive for long.*[6]

Therefore, creating a healthy heartbeat by combining your metrics with stories that illustrate vital behaviors is important. You're communicating to your organization two fundamental things:

---

6 [Doerr] p. 213

- This is what we want (e.g., the metric moves up or down)

- This is how we want to get there (e.g., stories or examples illustrating vital behavior)

The six hacks in this book are a great roadmap to help you find the stories you're looking for.

For example, you should be looking for examples of when teams tear down silos and build bridges with one another on behalf of the customer. Or look for examples of courage, when an employee exhibited a learning mindset over a knowing one, experimenting with a novel idea that went against conventional wisdom.

By consistently celebrating these moments and giving them visibility, you're communicating to the organization that you value these moments just as much as a spike in revenue. This can be an incredibly powerful motivator, inspiring employees to create customer-driven stories for themselves.

"Managers don't have to suffer the inefficiencies engendered by formal rules, procedures, and regulations," Andy Grove says. "[M]anagement has to develop and nurture the common set of values, objectives, and methods essential to the existence of trust. How do we do that? One way is by articulation, by spelling [them] out. The other even more important way is by example."[7]

Applying the Hack

Here are some suggestions for effectively measuring cultural change in your organization:

- Identify the current measurements that you're using to determine positive culture growth. For each measurement, ask yourselves, "Does this metric *multiply* our employees toward desired behaviors, or are they unnecessarily punitive and diminishing?"

- Consider how you're currently utilizing feedback from your employees. Has it been integrated in determining success, or is your organization overreliant on moving a single number? Ensure that you've diversified your measurements to include both quantitative and qualitative signals.

- As a team, have a brainstorming exercise to determine the set of vital behaviors that will indicate your culture is moving in the right direction. What actions would indicate that your employees are embracing a culture of awareness, curiosity, and courage? How might we count those behaviors when they happen?

---

7 [Wheatley]

- Conduct monthly, small-sample "pulse surveys" that check in on your culture's progress. You can ask employees to rate their experience on a Likert scale (e.g., strongly disagree versus strongly agree). You can pose statements for their agreement like:

  — I have access to customer data that helps me make decisions in a customer-driven way.

  — My team cares about customer feedback and actively integrates it into our decision making.

  — My manager encourages me to connect with customers and collect feedback.

  — We make product decisions based on what our customers want, not what our leadership wants.

  — I have a strong connection to our customers' motivations, needs, frustrations, and desires.

  — I have the tools I need to do my job effectively.

  — I'm proud to say I work at [company name].

  — I would recommend a friend or family member to work at [company name].

- Consider how you're using your measurements to create moments. When the organization or team achieves an objective, have a celebration and use that opportunity to inspire everyone with a more ambitious goal.

- Seek opportunities to highlight employees who are exhibiting vital behaviors and connect how their work is helping "move the needle" in a positive way. Bring teams up on stage during quarterly meetings and let them tell employees their stories in their own words.

In Conclusion

I sincerely hope you've had as much fun on this journey as I've had in sharing it with you. In conclusion, I want to give you a quick summary.

The Three Vital Behaviors

Throughout this entire book, I've given examples of the most fundamental behaviors that are required for any change effort. I encourage you to either use these behaviors or identify and name behaviors that will be important for your own change initiatives. As a reminder, here are the three vital behaviors for change:

Awareness

> The ability to identify our own assumptions and biases, not only about our customers, but each other, and understanding that we don't always have the complete picture in every situation.

Curiosity

> After you've become aware of your own assumptions, you must ask questions, dig deeper, and seek a continual understanding of the impact of your efforts.

Courage

> The bottom line is that change takes courage from all of us. It requires us to be willing to try something different and admit when our ideas might not be working. Building psychological safety isn't just management's job. It requires a commitment from all of us to engage in respectful behavior and support the process of learning, even when experiments prove our hypotheses wrong.

Hack #1: Establish a Common Language

In every culture, language is the tool we use to express our values, desires, and what matters to us most.

- If you change the language, you'll change the thinking, which will change the actions of your employees, which will ultimately change the values and culture of your organization (see Figure 2-1).

- A language of learning is a great foundation for a customer-driven culture. For DevDiv, "assumptions," "hypotheses," "experiments," and "sense-making" are terms we weave into our product reviews, customer development notes, and day-to-day operating language.

Hack #2: Build Bridges, Not Walls

To build exceptional products and services for your customers, your organization will need to treat building products like a team sport.

- Seek ways to improve cross-functional knowledge sharing. Review how knowledge is shared throughout your organization and identify ways to remove unnecessary barriers.

- Building a customer-driven culture is so much more than just improving customer relations. As your employees connect to customers, it's also an opportunity for them to connect to one another. Ensure that learning from customers is a shared experience for all product members, not just a select few experts.

- A customer-driven culture is one that values attitudes and passions over roles and responsibilities. Organizational structure is necessary for business operation, but your employees should be encouraged to try on other "hats." For example, a product manager should have the opportunity to talk to a customer with support from an account manager or user researcher.

- Avoid gatekeeping of knowledge and expertise. Experts should give of their knowledge and skills freely. It's not what you know that makes you valuable to your organization, it's your ability to learn and share that knowledge with your team members.

Hack #3: Encourage Learning versus Knowing

Throughout this book, I've suggested a positive correlation between an organization's willingness to learn and their ability to drive a customer-driven culture. Building great products for your customers requires an insatiable appetite to continuously learn about them.

- Celebrate learning, not failure. Not everything in your culture should be measured on whether it produced a successful product outcome. Certainly, developing product successes is critical for keeping a business going, but so is demonstrating that your organization is learning from its mistakes. Organizational growth is more nuanced and cannot be reduced to a simple pass/fail outcome. Be sure that you're spending time celebrating when your product teams encounter meaningful learnings, not just when they've met a product release deadline.

- You must actively work to create a space that is conducive to learning. Root out "know-it-all" behaviors by giving a platform for diverse voices, opinions, and perspectives to be shared.

- The quickest way to influence others is to genuinely invest in their success. If they believe that you're in it to help *them* win, they'll be much more likely to join you on your journey toward cultural transformation. Trust is everything when you're in the change business.

- Rather than shutting down alternative ideas, seek ways to build upon them. Modeling inclusive behavior, multiplying the passions and energy of those around you, and giving credit to others will not only gain you respect from your peers, it will also demonstrate what a culture that values learning looks like.

Hack #4: Build Leaders That Build Your Culture

Employees need to see what the new culture looks like. The best way to demonstrate that is by showcasing employees who are succeeding by applying the vital behaviors.

- Script the vital behaviors by removing barriers and roadblocks. Make it easy for employees to do the right thing and difficult to do the wrong thing. Evaluate your systems and tools and ensure that it's simple to begin engaging in the new culture.

- As a leader, what you say, what you spend your time on, and who you promote are powerful cues that tell employees what it means to belong to your organization. Reflect on the behaviors of your "star employees." Do they represent the values of the culture you're trying to build?

- Look for diverse voices, faces, behaviors, and roles when highlighting success in your organization. Spread recognition around and show that the pathway for success in your organization doesn't just come from shipping a product.

- Realize that there are key moments in the life cycle of an employee's career with your organization. Seek opportunities like employee onboarding, the kickoff of a new project, or an employee's retirement party to embed belonging cues and reinforce the values and commitments of your organization.

Hack #5: Meet Teams Where They Are

- Being a change agent requires that you must be "passionately pragmatic." Instead of fighting for a dogmatic adherence to your cultural initiatives, seek ways to make it easier for teams to change their behavior.

- Beyond salary and benefits, employees have shown that they are motivated by autonomy and mastery. In short, employees want to demonstrate that they're great at what they do. Create flexibility in your practices that allow teams to make the process of being customer driven their own.

- Empathize with your detractors. Showing that you're willing to listen to them and assume a positive intent will go a long way toward building trust.

- Rather than implementing costly new and expansive tools, where possible, consider taking advantage of tools that are already in place. Pick and choose your battles carefully and avoid getting sucked into meaningless battles that have more to do with ego than encouraging growth and learning.

- Focus and reorient existing energy. Rather than fight the team's motivations, seek ways to embrace team members and align them with your efforts. For example, if the team is ready to ship a feature, rather than block it because it hasn't tested it with customers, consider developing a plan that will allow the team to test it by collecting customer feedback after the feature has shipped.

Hack #6 Make Data Relatable

If you want to inspire others to action, you'll need more than just numbers and spreadsheets. The human mind is geared to process data *and* emotion. By ignoring the story of our customers, we lose vital information that helps us connect and empathize with them.

- Although telemetry and analytics can tell you *what* your customers are doing with your products and services, it will never tell you *why* they are doing it. Ensure that you're capturing their vivid experiences by engaging and talking with them.

- All great stories employ five essential patterns:

Simplicity
>They're easy to understand and share.

Unexpectedness
>They're memorable because they reveal something unexpected.

Concreteness
>They're clear and succinct. They don't involve too many ideas; they stick to one clear message.

Credibility
>They're believable and authentic.

Emotions
>They don't shy away from the emotions, sincere reactions, and honest feedback that connect us to our customers.

Thank You

Finally, Monty and I want to thank you, dear reader, for taking an interest in our journey. At Microsoft, we are committed to empowering every person and organization on the planet to achieve more. We hope that sharing these cultural hacks will empower you and your organization to connect with your customers in a way that allows you to empower them as well.

As Charles Darwin once said, "It is not the strongest of the species that survives, nor the most intelligent, but rather the one most adaptable to change."

On behalf of everyone in the Developer Division at Microsoft, I wish you the best on your journey of change as you connect and learn from your customers and one another.

References

[ABC13] ABC 13 Houston Texas. "King Buc-Ee's! Gas Station Crowned Highest-Rated Place to Use Restroom in the Nation." ABC13 Houston, May 17, 2018. *https://abc13.com/3487681/*.

[APA] "Are Zero Tolerance Policies Effective in the Schools?: An Evidentiary Review and Recommendations." *American Psychologist* 63, no. 9 (2008): 852–62. *https://doi.org/10.1037/0003-066X.63.9.852*.

[Alvarez] Alvarez, Cindy. *Lean Customer Development: Building Products Your Customers Will Buy*. Sebastopol, CA: O'Reilly Media, 2014.

[Ax] Ax, Joseph. "Bloomberg's Ban on Big Sodas Is Unconstitutional: Appeals Court." *Reuters*, July 30, 2013. *https://www.reuters.com/article/us-sodaban-lawsuit-idUSBRE96T0UT20130730*.

[Bigelow] Bigelow, Bruce. "#Hashtag This: How the Twitter Hashtag Caught Fire in San Diego." *Xconomy*, December 22, 2014. *https://xconomy.com/san-diego/2014/12/22/hashtag-this-how-the-twitter-hashtag-caught-fire-in-san-diego/*.

[Bishop] Bishop, Todd. "Exclusive: Satya Nadella Reveals Microsoft's New Mission Statement, Sees 'Tough Choices' Ahead." *GeekWire*, June 25, 2015. *https://www.geekwire.com/2015/exclusive-satya-nadella-reveals-microsofts-new-mission-statement-sees-more-tough-choices-ahead/*.

[Buckingham] Buckingham, Marcus, and Ashley Goodall. "The Feedback Fallacy." *Harvard Business Review*, March 1, 2019. *https://hbr.org/2019/03/the-feedback-fallacy*.

[Bulgarella] Bulgarella, Caterina. "Five Ps Pave The Way To Purpose At Microsoft." *Forbes*, July 11, 2019. *https://www.forbes.com/sites/caterinabulgarella/2019/06/11/five-ps-pave-the-way-to-purpose-at-microsoft/*.

[Bustillo] Bustillo, Miguel. "Roadside Stopper: Can Something Be Too Big in Texas?" *Wall Street Journal*, September 13, 2012, sec. US Page One. *https://www.wsj.com/articles/SB10000872396390444914904577623862863808508*.

[Carbonara] Carbonara, Peter. "How Two Texans Made Buc-Ee's Convenience Stores A Phenomenon." *Forbes*. Accessed April 20, 2019. *https://www.forbes.com/sites/petercarbonara/2017/08/22/buc-ees-game-of-porcelain-thrones/*.

[Carbonara-2] Carbonara, Peter. "Gaming the System: How A Traditional Manufacturer Opened Its Books and Turned Employees Into Millionaires." *Forbes*. Accessed June 1, 2019. *https://www.forbes.com/sites/petercarbonara/2017/04/18/gaming-the-system-how-one-manufacturing-company-saved-itself-with-radical-transparency-and-created-a-slew-of-blue-collar-millionaires/*.

[Chartrand] Chartrand, Tanya L., and John A. Bargh. "The Chameleon Effect: The Perception-Behavior Link and Social Interaction." *Journal of Personality and Social Psychology* 76, no. 6 (1999): 893–910.

[Clifford] Clifford, Catherine. "Elon Musk Hung out in the Netscape Lobby in the '90s Hoping to Get a Job, but Was Too Afraid to Talk to Anyone." CNBC, June 18, 2018. *https://www.cnbc.com/2018/06/18/how-elon-musk-tried-to-get-a-job-at-netscape-in-the-1990s.html.*

[Collins] Collins, Jim, and Jerry I. Porras. *Built to Last: Successful Habits of Visionary Companies.* 10th revised ed. New York: Harper Business, 2004.

[Cooper] Cooper, Matthew. "Poll: Most Americans Support Occupy Wall Street." *The Atlantic,* October 19, 2011. *https://www.theatlantic.com/politics/archive/2011/10/poll-most-americans-support-occupy-wall-street/246963/.*

[Cooperrider] Cooperrider, David, Frank Barrett, and Suresh Srivastava. "Social Construction and Appreciative Inquiry: A Journey in Organizational Theory." In *Management and Organization: Relational Alternatives to Individualism.* Ashgate Publishing, 1995.

[Coyle] Coyle, Daniel. *The Culture Code: The Secrets of Highly Successful Groups.* New York: Bantam, 2018.

[Doerr] Doerr, John. *Measure What Matters: How Google, Bono, and the Gates Foundation Rock the World with OKRs.* Portfolio, 2018.

[Dorsey] Dorsey, David. "Positive Deviant." *Fast Company,* November 30, 2000. *https://www.fastcompany.com/42075/positive-deviant.*

[DeGrassi] DeGrassi, Sandra, Whitney Botsford Morgan, Sarah Singletary, Wang (Irene) Yingchun, and Isaac Sabat. "Ethical Decision-Making: Group Diversity Holds the Key." Accessed April 30, 2019. *https://eds.b.ebscohost.com/ehost/pdfviewer/pdfviewer? vid=1&sid=1cdf7789-3eb8-4fb8-9d09-63fb5b456be4%40sessionmgr120.*

[Dreyfuss] Dreyfuss, Emily. "The Wikipedia for Spies—And Where It Goes From Here." *Wired,* March 10, 2017. *https://www.wired.com/2017/03/intellipedia-wikipedia-spies-much/.*

[Drucker] Drucker, Peter F. *The Practice of Management.* New York: Harper Business, 2006.

[Dyer] Dyer, Chris. *The Power of Company Culture: How Any Business Can Build a Culture That Improves Productivity, Performance and Profits.* United Kingdom; New York: Kogan Page, 2018.

[Edmondson] Edmondson, Amy C. "Learning From Mistakes Is Easier Said Than Done." *The Journal of Applied Behavioral Science* 40, no. 1 (March 2004): 66–90. *https://doi.org/10.1177/0021886304263849.*

[Epstein] Epstein, David. *Range: Why Generalists Triumph in a Specialized World.* New York: Riverhead Books, 2019.

[Field] Field, Anne. "Millennials Want Companies Mixing Mission And Money." *Forbes,* December 11, 2017. *https://www.forbes.com/sites/annefield/2017/12/11/millennials-want-companies-mixing-mission-and-money/.*

[Foley] Foley, Mary Jo. "Microsoft's New Mission Statement: No More Computer on Every Desk." ZDNet. Accessed April 4, 2019. *https://www.zdnet.com/article/microsofts-new-mission-statement-no-more-computer-on-every-desk/*.

[Fleming] Fleming, William. "Want Your Employees to Go Above and Beyond to Serve Your Customers? | LinkedIn." *LinkedIn* (blog), February 21, 2019. *https://www.linkedin.com/pulse/want-your-employees-go-above-beyond-serve-customers-william-fleming/?published=t*.

[Friedman] Friedman, Ron, PhD. *The Best Place to Work: The Art and Science of Creating an Extraordinary Workplace.* New York: Perigee, 2015.

[Geary] Geary, James. *I Is an Other: The Secret Life of Metaphor and How It Shapes the Way We See the World.* New York: Harper Perennial, 2012.

[Gandhi] Gandhi, Mohandas Karamchand. *The Collected Works of Mahatma Gandhi: (11 April, 1910 - 12 July, 1911), Volume 11.* Andesite Press, 2015.

[Grant] Grant, Adam, and Sheryl Sandberg. *Originals: How Non-Conformists Move the World.* New York: Viking, 2016.

[Greenwood] Greenwood, Max. "Five Years to the Top: Microsoft's Software Boss Julia Liuson." *Techvibes,* April 9, 2019. *https://techvibes.com/2019/04/09/five-years-to-the-top-microsofts-software-boss-julia-liuson.*

[Grynbaum] Grynbaum, Michael M. "New York's Ban on Big Sodas Is Rejected by Final Court." *The New York Times,* June 26, 2014, sec. New York. *https://www.nytimes.com/2014/06/27/nyregion/city-loses-final-appeal-on-limiting-sales-of-large-sodas.html.*

[Grynbaum-2] Grynbaum, Michael M., and Marjorie Connelly. "Most New Yorkers Oppose Bloomberg's Soda Ban." *The New York Times,* August 22, 2012, sec. N.Y. / Region. *https://www.nytimes.com/2012/08/23/nyregion/most-new-yorkers-oppose-bloombergs-soda-ban.html.*

[Hansen] Hansen, Morten. *Great at Work: How Top Performers Do Less, Work Better, and Achieve More.* New York: Simon & Schuster, 2018.

[Heath] Heath, Chip, and Dan Heath. *Switch: How to Change Things When Change Is Hard.* New York: Crown Business, 2010.

[Heath-2] Heath, Chip, and Dan Heath. *The Power of Moments: Why Certain Experiences Have Extraordinary Impact.* New York: Simon & Schuster, 2017.

[Helm] Helm, Burt. "The 5 Unexpected Benefits of Open-Book Management." *Inc,* October 12, 2013. *https://www.inc.com/burt-helm/five-benefits-of-opening-your-books.html.*

[Influencer] Patterson, Kerry, Joseph Grenny, David Maxfield, Ron McMillan, and Al Switzler. *Influencer: The New Science of Leading Change.* New York: McGraw-Hill, 2007.

[Intellipedia] "Intellipedia." In *Wikipedia,* November 4, 2018. *https://en.wikipedia.org/w/index.php?title=Intellipedia&oldid=867303816.*

[Kelley] Kelley, Tom, and Jonathan Littman. *The Ten Faces of Innovation: IDEO's Strategies for Beating the Devil's Advocate and Driving Creativity Throughout Your Organization.* New York: Currency/Doubleday, 2005.

[Kelly] Kelly, Lois, and Carmen Medina. *Rebels at Work: A Handbook for Leading Change from Within*. Edited by Debra Cameron. Sebastopol, CA: O'Reilly Media, 2014.

[Kennedy] Kennedy, Bian, and Meg Hefferon. "What Americans Know About Science." *Pew Research Center Science & Society* (blog), March 28, 2019. *https://www.pewresearch.org/science/2019/03/28/what-americans-know-about-science/*.

[Konrad] Konrad, Alex. "Exclusive CEO Interview: Satya Nadella Reveals How Microsoft Got Its Groove Back." *Forbes*, December 10, 2018. *https://www.forbes.com/sites/alexkonrad/2018/12/10/exclusive-ceo-interview-satya-nadella-reveals-how-microsoft-got-its-groove-back/*.

[Krout] Krout, Kelly. Interview with Kelly Krout, August 27, 2019.

[Liuson] Liuson, Julia. Interview with Julia Liuson, July 29, 2019.

[Lowdermilk-Rich] Lowdermilk, Travis, and Jessica Rich. *The Customer-Driven Playbook: Converting Customer Feedback into Successful Products*. Sebastopol, CA: O'Reilly Media, 2017.

[MacKenzie] MacKenzie, Kristin. "The Building Blocks of a Great Company, According to Buc-Ee's Founder." *Mays Impacts*. Accessed April 20, 2019. *https://mays-tamu-edu.cdn.ampproject.org/v/s/mays.tamu.edu/news/2012/09/25/the-building-blocks-of-a-great-company/amp/?usqp=mq331AQCCAE%3D&amp_js_v=0.1*.

[McLeod] McLeod, Poppy Lauretta, Sharon Alisa Lobel, and Taylor H. Cox. "Ethnic Diversity and Creativity in Small Groups." *Small Group Research* 27, no. 2 (May 1, 1996): 248–64. *https://doi.org/10.1177/1046496496272003*.

[McMillan] McMillan, Chase, and Kerry Patterson. "No Condom, No Sex: Why Thailand's 100% Condom Campaign Has Been an Unparalleled Success." Brigham Young University, September 12, 2013. *http://jur.byu.edu/?p=5599*.

[Monarth] Monarth, Harrison. "The Irresistible Power of Storytelling as a Strategic Business Tool." *Harvard Business Review*, March 11, 2014. *https://hbr.org/2014/03/the-irresistible-power-of-storytelling-as-a-strategic-business-tool*.

[Montgomery] Montgomery, John. Interview with John Montgomery, September 18, 2019.

[Montgomery-2] Montgomery, John. "Rethinking How We Interview in Microsoft's Developer Division." *Medium*, January 28, 2019. *https://blog.usejournal.com/rethinking-how-we-interview-in-microsofts-developer-division-8f404cfd075a*.

[Mosendz] Mosendz, Polly. "Microsoft's CEO Sent a 3,187-Word Memo and We Read It So You Don't Have To." *The Atlantic*, July 10, 2014. *https://www.theatlantic.com/technology/archive/2014/07/microsofts-ceo-sent-a-3187-word-memo-and-we-read-it-so-you-dont-have-to/374230/*.

[Nadella] Nadella, Satya, Greg Shaw, and Jill Tracie Nichols. *Hit Refresh: The Quest to Rediscover Microsoft's Soul and Imagine a Better Future for Everyone*. Harper Business, 2019.

[Nap] Medicine National Academies of Sciences. *How People Learn II: Learners, Contexts, and Cultures*. Washington, DC: National Academies Press, 2018.

[Nusca] Nusca, Andrew. "Inside Microsoft's Plan to Reconquer the World." *Fortune*. Accessed January 27, 2019. *http://fortune.com/microsoft-fortune-500-cloud-computing/*.

[Oatley] Oatley, Keith. "Why Fiction May Be Twice as True as Fact: Fiction as Cognitive and Emotional Simulation." *Review of General Psychology* 3, no. 2 (1999): 101–17. *https://doi.org/10.1037/1089-2680.3.2.101.*

[Ralph] Ralph, Ben. "How to Stop UX Research Being a Blocker." *Medium*, May 12, 2018. *https://medium.com/beakerandflint/how-to-stop-ux-research-being-a-blocker-225d91105de8.*

[Ranger] Ranger, Steve. "Windows 8: Why Microsoft's Giant Gamble Didn't Pay Off." ZDNet. Accessed April 20, 2019. *https://www.zdnet.com/article/windows-8-why-microsofts-giant-gamble-didnt-pay-off/.*

[Richard] Richard, Orlando C. "Racial Diversity, Business Strategy, and Firm Performance: A Resource-Based View." *Academy of Management Journal* 43, no. 2 (April 1, 2000): 164–77. *https://doi.org/10.5465/1556374.*

[Roam] Roam, Dan. *Blah Blah Blah: What to Do When Words Don't Work.* New York: Portfolio, 2011.

[SafetyRules] SafetyNurse1968. "The Wrong Dose - A True Story of Medication Error." allnurses.com. Accessed June 4, 2019. *https://allnurses.com/the-wrong-dose-a-t677840/.*

[Salva] Salva, Ryan. Interview with Ryan Salva, June 5, 2019.

[Schein] Schein, Edgar H., and Peter Schein. *Organizational Culture and Leadership.* Hoboken, New Jersey: Wiley, 2016.

[Sharot] Sharot, Tali. *The Influential Mind: What the Brain Reveals About Our Power to Change Others.* New York: Henry Holt and Co., 2017.

[Silver-1] Silver, Amanda. Interview with Amanda Silver, October 22, 2019.

[Silver-2] Silver, Amanda. Interview with Amanda Silver, August 13, 2019.

[Stephens] Stephens, Greg J., Lauren J. Silbert, and Uri Hasson. "Speaker–Listener Neural Coupling Underlies Successful Communication." *Proceedings of the National Academy of Sciences of the United States of America* 107, no. 32 (August 10, 2010): 14425–30. *https://doi.org/10.1073/pnas.1008662107.*

[Suhartono] Suhartono, Muktita, and Richard C. Paddock. "Soccer Team Is Found Alive in Thailand Cave Rescue." *The New York Times*, July 2, 2018, sec. World. *https://www.nytimes.com/2018/07/02/world/asia/thailand-boys-rescued.html.*

[Sun] "Microsoft CEO Takes Launch Break with the Sun-Times." *Chicago Sun Times*, December 11, 2001. *http://web.archive.org/web/20011211130654* (*http://web.archive.org/web/20011211130654/http:/www.suntimes.com/output/tech/cst-fin-micro01.html*).

[Sunstein] Sunstein, Cass R. "Amazon Is Right That Disagreement Results in Better Decisions." *Harvard Business Review*, August 18, 2015. *https://hbr.org/2015/08/amazon-is-right-that-disagreement-results-in-better-decisions.*

[Tate-Wang] Tate, Emily. "You Don't Own the Voice of the Customer by Tricia Wang." *Mind the Product* (blog), August 30, 2019. *https://www.mindtheproduct.com/2019/08/you-dont-own-the-voice-of-the-customer-by-tricia-wang/.*

[Tate-Portigal] Tate, Emily. "Great User Research (for Non-Researchers) by Steve Portigal." *Mind the Product* (blog), September 13, 2019. *https://www.mindtheproduct.com/great-user-research-for-non-researchers-by-steve-portigal/*.

[Tiku] Tiku, Nitasha. "Microsoft Employees Protest Treatment of Women to CEO Nadella." *Wired*, April 4, 2019. *https://www.wired.com/story/microsoft-employees-protest-treatment-women-ceo-nadella/*.

[Values] Center for Values-Driven Leadership. *Creating Psychological Safety at Work in a Knowledge Economy | Amy Edmondson, Harvard.* Accessed June 4, 2019. *https://www.youtube.com/watch?time_continue=120&v=KU01QwVcCv0*.

[Vlaskovits] Vlaskovits, Patrick. "Henry Ford, Innovation, and That 'Faster Horse' Quote." *Harvard Business Review*, August 29, 2011. *https://hbr.org/2011/08/henry-ford-never-said-the-fast*.

[Warren] Warren, Tom. "Microsoft Writes off $7.6 Billion from Nokia Deal, Announces 7,800 Job Cuts." *The Verge*, July 8, 2015. *https://www.theverge.com/2015/7/8/8910999/microsoft-job-cuts-2015-nokia-write-off*.

[Waters] Waters, John K. "New Release 'Cadence' Begins with Visual Studio 2012 Update 2 -." *Visual Studio Magazine*, May 10, 2013. *https://visualstudiomagazine.com/articles/2013/05/10/new-visual-studio-release-cadence-begins.aspx*.

[Wheatley] Wheatley, Margaret, and Myron Kellner-Rogers. "What Do We Measure and Why? Questions About The Uses of Measurement." *Journal for Strategic Performance Measurement*, June 1999. *https://www.margaretwheatley.com/wp-content/uploads/2014/12/What-Do-We-Measure-and-Why.pdf*.

[WHO] World Health Organization. "Thailand's New Condom Crusade." *Bulletin of the World Health Organization* 88, no. 6 (June 1, 2010): 404–5. *https://doi.org/10.2471/BLT.10.010610*.

[Whorf] Whorf, Benjamin Lee, John B. Carroll, and Stuart Chase. *Language, Thought, and Reality: Selected Writings of Benjamin Lee Whorf.* Mansfield Centre, CT: Martino Fine Books, 2011.

[Zak] Zak, Elana. "How Twitter's Hashtag Came to Be." *WSJ* (blog), October 3, 2013. *https://blogs.wsj.com/digits/2013/10/03/how-twitters-hashtag-came-to-be/*.

[Zak-Paul] Zak, Paul J. "Why Your Brain Loves Good Storytelling." *Harvard Business Review*, October 28, 2014. *https://hbr.org/2014/10/why-your-brain-loves-good-storytelling*.

Photo Credit

Huggins, Stacey. "Buc-Ee's." Flickr, September 29, 2010. *https://www.flickr.com/photos/stacey-huggins/5051014221/*.

Appendix

Here are some additional resources that you might find helpful.

Books You Should Read

Monty and I are voracious readers. We absolutely love books and, if you ever meet us in person, there's a good chance we'll encourage you to borrow one.

Earlier, we mentioned the value of creating a library within your team room. Although we're eternally grateful that you chose our book, we would be remiss if we didn't suggest adding the following texts to your library as well. These authors deserve the lion's share of the credit for our learnings. Without them, we would not have reached the clarity and articulation for our own cultural transformation.

Accelerate: Building and Scaling High Performing Technology Organizations by Nicole Forsgren, PhD, Jez Humble, and Gene Kim. Published by IT Revolution Press, 2018.

Be Fearless: 5 Principles for a Life of Breakthroughs and Purpose by Jean Case. Published by Simon & Schuster, 2019.

Blitzscaling: The Lightning-Fast Path to Building Massively Valuable Companies by Reid Hoffman and Chris Yeh. Published by Currency, 2018.

Built to Last: Successful Habits of Visionary Companies by Jim Collins. Published by Harper Business, 1994.

Change by Design: How Design Thinking Transforms Organizations and Inspires Innovation by Tim Brown. Published by Harper Business, 2009.

Crossing the Chasm by Geoffrey Moore. Published by Harper Business, 2014.

Dealing with Darwin: How Great Companies Innovate at Every Phase of Their Evolution by Geoffrey Moore. Published by Portfolio, 2005.

Design-Driven Innovation: Changing the Rules of Competition by Radically Innovating What Things Mean by Roberto Verganti. Published by Harvard Business Press, 2009.

Draw to Win: A Crash Course on How to Lead, Sell, and Innovate with Your Visual Mind by Dan Roam. Published by Portfolio, 2016.

Drive: The Surprising Truth About What Motivates Us by Daniel Pink. Published by River-head Books, 2011.

Ego is the Enemy by Ryan Holiday. Published by Portfolio, 2016.

Good to Great: Why Some Companies Make the Leap and Others Don't by Jim Collins. Published by Harper Business, 2001.

Great at Work: How Top Performers Do Less, Work Better, and Achieve More by Morten Hansen. Published by Simon & Schuster, 2018.

Grit: The Power of Passion and Perseverance by Angela Duckworth. Published by Scribner, 2018.

Hacking Growth: How Today's Fastest-Growing Companies Drive Breakout Success by Sean Ellis and Morgan Brown. Published by Currency, 2017.

Hit Refresh: The Quest to Rediscover Microsoft's Soul and Imagine a Better Future for Everyone by Satya Nadella. Published by Harper Business, 2017.

If I Understood You, Would I Have This Look on My Face?: My Adventures in the Art and Science of Relating and Communicating by Alan Alda. Published by Radom House, 2018.

Influencer: The New Science of Leading Change by Joseph Grenny, Kerry Patterson, David Maxfield, Ron McMillan, and Al Switzler. Published by McGraw-Hill Education, 2013.

Leading Change by John Kotter. Published by Harvard Business Review Press, 2012.

Lean Customer Development: Building Products Your Customers Will Buy by Cindy Alvarez. Published by O'Reilly Media, 2017.

Made to Stick: Why Some Ideas Survive and Others Die by Chip and Dan Heath. Published by Random House, 2007.

Mapping Innovation: A Playbook for Navigating a Disruptive Age by Greg Satell. Published by McGraw-Hill Education, 2017.

Measure What Matters: How Google, Bono, and the Gates Foundation Rock the World with OKRs by John Doerr. Published by Portfolio, 2018.

Mindset: The New Psychology of Success by Carol Dweck. Published by Ballantine Books, 2007.

Multipliers: How the Best Leaders Make Everyone Smarter by Liz Wiseman. Published by Harper Business, 2017.

Organizational Culture and Leadership by Edgar Schein. Published by Wiley, 2016.

Originals: How Non-Conformists Move the World by Adam Grant. Published by Penguin Books, 2017.

Radical Candor: Be a Kick-Ass Boss Without Losing Your Humanity by Kim Scott. Published by St. Martin's Press, 2017.

Rebels at Work: A Handbook for Leading Change from Within by Lois Kelly and Carmen Medina. Published by O'Reilly Media, 2014.

Show and Tell: How Everybody Can Make Extraordinary Presentations by Dan Roam. Published by Portfolio, 2016.

Switch: How to Change Things When Change is Hard by Chip and Dan Heath. Published by Crown Business, 2010.

Team of Teams: New Rules of Engagement for a Complex World by General Stanley McChrystal. Published by Penguin Business, 2015.

The Best Place to Work: The Art and Science of Creating an Extraordinary Workplace by Ron Friedman, PhD. Published by Perigee, 2015.

The Culture Code: The Secrets of Highly Successful Groups by Daniel Coyle. Published by Bantam, 2018.

The Entrepreneurial Mindset: Strategies for Continuously Creating Opportunity in an Age of Uncertainty by Rita McGrath and Ian MacMillan. Published by Harvard Business Review Press, 2000.

The Heart of Change: Real-Life Stories of How People Change Their Organizations by John Kotter and Dan Cohen. Published by Harvard Business Review Press, 2012.

The Innovator's Dilemma: When New Technologies Cause Great Firms to Fail by Clayton Christensen. Harvard Business Review Press, 2016.

The Innovator's DNA: Mastering the Five Skills of Disruptive Innovators by Jeff Dyer, Hal Gregersen, and Clayton Christensen. Published by Harvard Business Review Press, 2011.

The Innovator's Solution: Creating and Sustaining Successful Growth by Clayton Christensen and Michael Raynor. Published by Harvard Business Review Press, 2013.

The Lean Startup: How Today's Entrepreneurs Use Continuous Innovation to Create Radically Successful Businesses by Eric Ries. Published by Currency, 2011.

The Obstacle Is the Way: The Timeless Art of Turning Trials into Triumph by Ryan Holiday. Published by Portfolio, 2014.

The Power of Company Culture: How Any Business Can Build a Culture that Improves Productivity, Performance and Profits by Chris Dyer. Published by Kogan Page, 2018.

The Power of Moments: Why Certain Experiences Have Extraordinary Impact by Chip and Dan Heath. Published by Simon & Schuster, 2017.

The Practice of Management by Peter Drucker. Published by Harper Business, 1993 (originally published in 1954).

The Storyteller's Secret: From TED Speakers to Business Legends, Why Some Ideas Catch On and Others Don't by Carmine Gallo. Published by St. Martin's Griffin, 2017.

The Ten Faces of Innovation: IDEO's Strategies for Beating the Devil's Advocate and Driving Creativity Throughout Your Organization by Tom Kelley with Jonathan Littman. Published by Currency/Doubleday, 2005.

Trillion Dollar Coach: The Leadership Playbook of Silicon Valley's Bill Campbell by Erich Schmidt, Jonathan Rosenberg, and Alan Eagle. Published by Harper Business, 2019.

Figure A-1. Just a portion of the books that inspired the one you're reading now

Useful Maxims

In his book, *The Culture Code: The Secrets of Highly Successful Groups*, author Daniel Coyle discusses how great teams have maxims. These are short sayings that embody the belonging cues of what it means to be part of the team or organization. Monty and I just *love* maxims, because they're a shortcut to bigger themes and ideas. We find ourselves using these little statements over and over when sharing our journey, expressing our learning, and encouraging others to join us on our journey.

If you ever leaf through any of our books, you'll find these statements highlighted, tagged, and underlined. In our view, there's nothing better than a short, pithy statement that captures the essence of a big idea.

In fact, in our culture room (see Chapter 1), we covered the wall with some of our favorites that we've come across over the years. I'll list them here, without explanation. This way, you can reflect and find your own meaning in them.

HACK #1: USE A COMMON LANGUAGE

- Use a language of learning.
- Change the language and you'll change the thinking, which will change the actions and behaviors and, ultimately, change the culture.
- Language should connect the board room to the team room, and vice versa.
- Lean engineering is based on a language of learning.

HACK #2: BUILD BRIDGES, NOT WALLS

- Lean = Continuous and Collaborative learning.
- It's not about a few learnings on behalf of the many; it's about empowering everyone to learn.
- Great cultures build "generalists with superpowers."
- Maintaining zero distance between the customer and each other.
- Give knowledge away freely.
- Working with others, for others.
- Win as one.
- Work the team, then the problem.
- Fill the gaps between people.

- Bridge builders round up, not down.

HACK #3: ENCOURAGE LEARNING VERSUS KNOWING

- A customer-driven culture is rooted in continuous learning.
- Have courage to divorce yourself from your solution.
- Invalidated hypotheses are just as valuable as validated ones.
- Push for high-tempo experimentation.
- Value and promote small-batch learning.
- Reward learning over being proven right.
- You want to "de-risk" your decisions, not try and be "bulletproof."
- Constantly challenge your assumptions.
- Learning happens when we trip over the truth.
- Some people need the permission to be empathetic.

HACK #4: BUILD LEADERS THAT BUILD YOUR CULTURE

- Help others fall into the pit of *success*.
- The fastest way to gain influence with someone is to help them get promoted.
- If you don't name the behavior, you can't acknowledge it or aspire to it.
- Build belonging cues into everything you do.
- Help your people do heroic things.
- To care about people, you must care about people.

HACK #5: MEET TEAMS WHERE THEY ARE

- Make it easy to do the right thing and difficult to do the wrong thing.
- You can't be dealt a hand that you can't play.
- One size fits one.
- Value conversation over documentation.

- Leverage *their* energy.
- Make the charitable assumption.
- Be passionately pragmatic.
- Coach it, from the board room—to the team room.
- Culture Growth = Desire – Friction.
- Be a coach, not just a teacher.
- Only coach the coachable.
- Leading people becomes a lot more effective when you care about the people you're trying to lead.

HACK #6: MAKE DATA RELATABLE

- Strive for grounded confidence.
- Customer connections should be the new currency.
- When telling a story, lead with your big surprises.
- Avoid being data rich and action poor.
- There are three faces of customer value: functional, social, and emotional.
- Never settle for the *what* without the *why*.
- IQ + EQ = CQ or (Intelligence Quotient) + (Emotional Intelligence) = (Customer Intelligence).

Index

M

About the Authors

Travis Lowdermilk

Travis Lowdermilk is a UX researcher, author, designer, storyteller, prototyper, coder, maker, mentor, and doer. Currently, he works for Microsoft's Developer Division, helping teams make tools and platforms for software developers. Travis has a B.S. in Information Systems from California State University, Fresno and an M.S. in Human-Computer Interaction from DePaul University. His background is a unique blend of systems-thinking, human factors, user research, design, and engineering.

Travis is especially passionate about helping product teams connect with their customers to uncover unmet needs and build innovative products. He's had the opportunity to work with product teams from all over the world, sharing his expertise and inspiring product makers to drive customer connection and empathy into the center of their product making process.

He's also the coauthor of *The Customer-Driven Playbook* and the author of *User-Centered Design* (O'Reilly).

In his spare time, Travis enjoys photography, reading, writing, and exploring new technologies. He lives in the Seattle area with his wife Jackie, two sons Noah and Jackson, their dog Muggles, and Jake the cat (when Jake decides they are worthy of his presence).

To learn more about Travis, visit www.travislowdermilk.com or follow him on Twitter (@tlowdermilk).

Monty Hammontree

Monty Hammontree is the Partner Director of User Experience Research for Microsoft's developer tools and platforms division. He has over 30 years of industry experience in product design and user research management. In recent years Monty has been at the forefront of the formation and adoption of "lean" customer, product, and business development best practices within Microsoft. A primary theme of his career is the development and utilization of team-based techniques for uncovering innovation opportunities, exploring creative concepts, visualizing solution alternatives, and evaluating/refining candidate solutions.

Monty lives near Microsoft's main campus in Redmond Washington with his wife Amy. His five children, now grown, and six grandchildren are the pride of his life and his never-ending fountain of youth. He holds a PhD in Human Factors Engineering from Old Dominion University.

O'REILLY®

There's much more where this came from.

Experience books, videos, live online training courses, and more from O'Reilly and our 200+ partners—all in one place.

Learn more at oreilly.com/online-learning